Pelican Shared Writing

Fiction Teacher's Book 3

Wendy Body

Series Editor: Wendy Body

Pearson Education Limited
Edinburgh Gate
Harlow
Essex
CM20 2JE
England and Associated Companies throughout the World

ISBN 0582 48837 0
First published 2001
Second impression 2002

Printed in Great Britain by Scotprint, Haddington
Designed by AMR, Bramley, Hants

The Publisher's policy is to use paper manufactured from sustainable forests.

Longman
Edinburgh Gate
Harlow, Essex

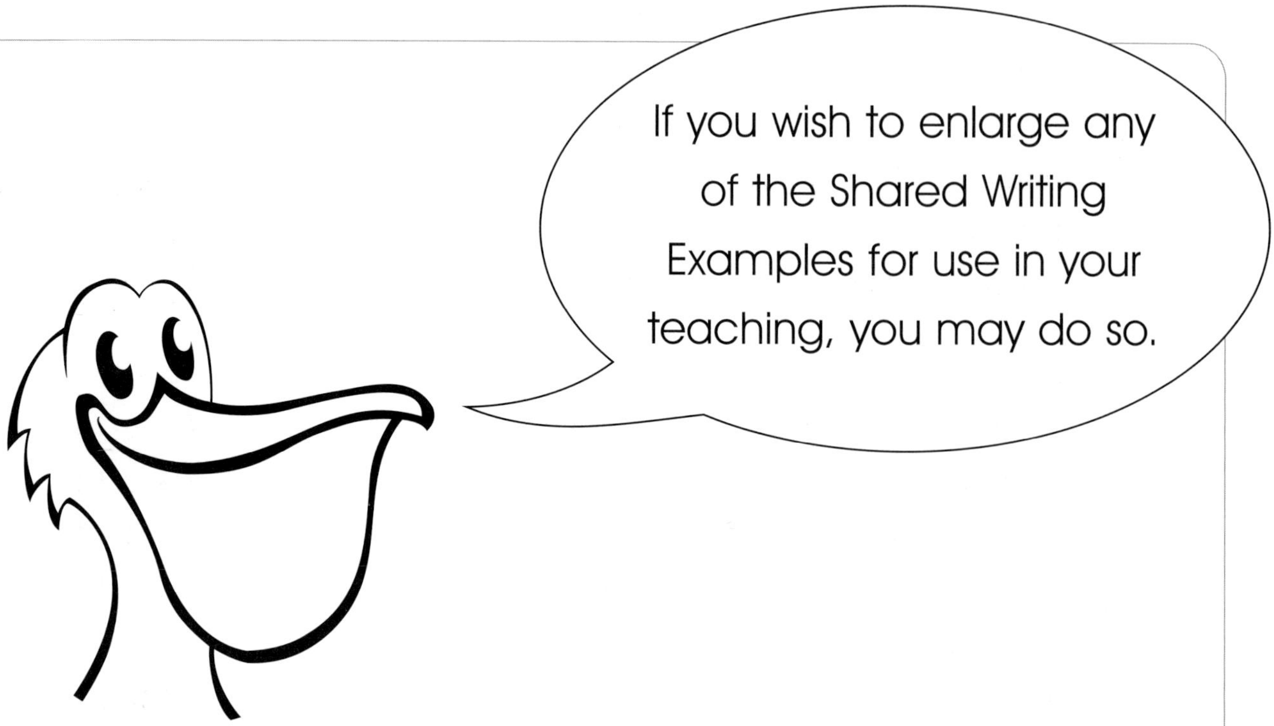
If you wish to enlarge any of the Shared Writing Examples for use in your teaching, you may do so.

Contents

Year 3 Fiction Summary Chart

Text in Resource Book	Text level Objective	Sentence level Objective Links	Unit of work
Term 1 Unit 1 Describing Settings	**T11**: to develop the use of settings in own stories	**S12**: to demarcate the end of a sentence with a full stop	Write descriptions based on models
Term 1 Unit 2 Writing Dialogue	**T10**: to write own passages of dialogue	**S7**: conventions of speech punctuation **S8**: to use the term 'speech marks'	Complete the dialogue
Term 1 Unit 3 Imaginative Comparisons	**T13**: to write imaginative comparisons		Write imaginative comparisons
Term 1 Unit 4 Short story: *I Spy ...*	**T15**: to write simple playscripts based on own reading	**S11**: to write in complete sentences	Change the story into a playscript
Term 1 Unit 5 Short story: *I Spy ...*	non-specific		Revise a piece of writing
Term 1 Unit 6 Shape poems: *Sleeping; Lamp-post*	**T14**: to invent ... a range of shape poems	**S13**: to use commas to separate items in a list	Write shape poems
Term 1 Unit 7 Openings Endings	**T12**: to investigate ... story openings and endings		Write examples of openings and endings
Term 1 Unit 8 Writing a Story in Paragraphs	**T16**: to begin to organise stories into paragraphs	**S7**: the basic conventions of speech punctuation	Write a story in paragraphs
Term 2 Unit 9 Extract from *Ant and Grasshopper*	**T7**: to describe and sequence key incidents in a variety of ways	**S6** & **S7**: the use of commas	Describe and sequence key incidents
Term 2 Unit 10 Extract from *Ant and Grasshopper*	**T10**: to write alternative sequels to traditional stories		Write alternative sequels
Term 2 Unit 11 *My Uncle Paul of Pimlico*	**T11**: to write new or extended verses for performance	**S8**: capitalisation in new lines of poetry	Write an additional verse

Term 2 Unit 12 Extract from *Cinderella*	**T9**: to write a story plan for own traditional tale, substituting different characters, settings; changing the setting		Change characters or plan own story
Term 2 Unit 13 Writing Character Portraits	**T8**: to write portraits of characters and present them in a variety of ways	**S2** & **S3**: experimenting with the impact of different adjectives; to use the term adjective appropriately	Write character portraits from pictures
Term 2 Unit 14 Plan the Story!	**T6**: to plan main points as a structure for story writing		Write a story plan for a traditional story
Term 3 Unit 15 Writing a Story in Chapters	**T13**: to write more extended stories … and set out in simple chapters	**S4**: to use speech marks and other dialogue punctuation appropriately	Make a detailed plan and write the story
Term 3 Unit 16 Writing a Story in Chapters	**T12**: to write a first person account	**S2**: first and third person forms of pronouns	Change a third person account into the first person
Term 3 Unit 17 *Mud* *Peter Piper*	**T15**: to write poetry that uses sound to create effects		Write sound effect poems
Term 3 Unit 18 *Jack and the Beanstalk:* a story plan	**T10**: to plot a sequence of episodes modelled on a known story as a plan for writing		Plan a story
Term 3 Unit 19 *Jack and the Beanstalk:* a story plan	**T11**: to write openings to stories or chapters ... to focus on language to create effects	**S5**: how sentences can be joined in more complex ways	Write a chapter opening
Term 3 Unit 20 Writing a Review	**T14**: to write book reviews for a specified audience, based on evaluations of plot, characters and language		Make notes and write a review

Introduction

What is *Pelican Shared Writing*?

Pelican Shared Writing is an easy-to-use resource for teaching shared writing. It comprises ten packs: one Fiction and one Non-Fiction pack for each year group for Years 2, 3, 4, 5 and 6. Each pack contains:

- one *Writing Resource Book*
- one *Teacher's Book* with copymasters
- a large sheet of acetate and a Pelican page clip.

Each *Writing Resource Book* offers 20 units of work which cover all the NLS writing composition objectives for the year group. Each writing composition objective forms one unit of work. Links are also made to appropriate sentence level objectives.

Although *Pelican Shared Writing* stands alone, it has links to *Pelican Guided Reading and Writing* in terms of objectives and tasks and there are content links to *Pelican Big Books*.

The *Writing Resource Books*

- Each 48-page big book is split into three parts – one for each term's teaching objectives.
- Shared writing is rooted in shared reading, and so the *Writing Resource Book* contains the texts which not only provide the starting point for writing, but also act as models of the genre to be studied. Story plans and writing frames are sometimes included as well.
- Quotes about the writing process from professional children's writers feature on the inside back cover of some of the *Fiction Writing Resource Books* to initiate discussions on writing.
- Each book comes with a large sheet of acetate and a Pelican page clip for text marking and writing.

The *Teacher's Books*

The *Teacher's Book* in each pack contains:

- teaching pages for each unit of work with detailed, step-by-step advice on what to do in each shared writing session. There are also examples of completed activities which teachers can use to guide the class in composing a text. Units will usually take more than one shared writing session to complete.
- a small number of copymasters e.g. writing frames, character planners. These are for general use and can also be applied to other texts and writing activities
- copymaster versions of all the *Writing Resource Book* texts. These can be used to make overhead transparencies and in instances where it is helpful for children to have their own copy of a text e.g. for annotation.

The *Non-Fiction Teacher's Book* has a summary of links to other areas of the curriculum on the last page.

Teaching Shared Writing

Pelican Shared Writing complements the National Literacy Strategy's *Grammar for Writing* guidance. *Pelican Shared Writing* concentrates on delivering the text level writing composition objectives whereas *Grammar for Writing* concentrates on sentence level objectives. *Pelican Shared Writing* adopts a similar approach to shared writing which may be summarised as follows:

Key features of shared writing

- Make explicit how purpose and audience determine form and style.
- Link the writing to specific objectives.
- Rehearse sentences orally before writing.
- Discuss and explain alternatives and choices.
- Keep rereading to maintain flow, meaning and consistency.
- Involve children in the revision and editing.

Shared Writing Techniques:

Teacher demonstration

The teacher composes and writes, modelling for children how to compose a particular text type or tackle a writing activity. He/she thinks aloud, rehearses choices before writing, explains choices and makes changes. The children do not contribute to the composition but they are invited to offer opinions on, for example, the choice of words or sentence construction. Demonstration time will vary according to the text and children's competence, but avoid spending too long – children need to try things for themselves.

Teacher scribing

The teacher acts as scribe and builds on the initial demonstration by asking the children to make contributions to the composition or task. The teacher guides, focuses, explains and challenges the contributions e.g. *Why did you choose that word? That's a really good sentence construction because ...* While children could make their contributions orally by putting up their hands, it is preferable for them to use whiteboards (in pairs or individually), which ensures participation by all children. It is also advisable to take "time out", i.e. children turn to each other in pairs and discuss possibilities for 30 seconds or so.

Supported composition

Supported composition is preparation for independent writing. Children compose a limited amount of text using whiteboards or notebooks – in pairs or individually. Their alternatives are reviewed and discussed and choices and changes made. Some differentiation can be achieved by seating children in their ability groups and asking one group to compose one sentence orally, another to write one or two sentences and a third to write several sentences. Supported composition will enable you to identify those children who will need to repeat or continue the task in guided writing i.e. those who need greater support.

Shared writing is the most powerful means of improving and developing children's writing skills. But they will not develop into proficient writers unless, firstly, they are given sufficient TIME to practise the skills and craft of writing for themselves, and secondly, they receive the FEEDBACK which will help them evaluate what they have done and learn from it.

Teaching a *Pelican Shared Writing* unit of work

Support for each step will be found on the teaching pages

Discussing the Text for each unit

- Introduce the task and the objective
- Read the text in the Resource Book with the class and discuss the content
- Draw out features of the genre

↓

Shared Writing

- Demonstrate or model the particular features of the writing
- Scribe and guide the pupils' contributions
- Continue with supported composition by children working in pairs
- Check the children's learning

↓

Independent Writing

- Children complete the writing task.
- They consolidate their learning by carrying out another similar task.

↓

Checking the Objective

- Determine children's understanding of the objective and how far they can apply their knowledge by evaluating their writing.

↓

Revisiting the Objective

- If needs be, repeat the whole process using the suggested activity.

Note: A *Pelican Shared Writing* CD-ROM is available for use alongside each year's work. For further details, please see the section on ICT overleaf.

ICT and *Pelican Shared Writing*

ICT may be used by all pupils to support writing skills. The word processor or desktop publishing package can enable the child to focus on the development of ideas and the manipulation of the written word without the physical constraints imposed by the handwriting process. The ease of editing, the spell-checking facilities and the ability to move text around the page make ICT support programs valuable tools to include within the writing repertoire. Writing tasks offer the ideal opportunity to integrate and apply those ICT skills being developed in the ICT curriculum.

Almost any writing task may be approached using ICT as an optional writing tool. These writing tasks will offer strong links with the ICT curriculum, which aims that pupils should:

- 'develop their ability to apply their IT capability and ICT to support their use of language and communication'
- 'pass on ideas by communicating, presenting and exchanging information'
- 'develop language skills eg in systematic writing and in presenting their own ideas'
- 'be creative and persistent'
- 'recognise the strengths and limitations of ICT'

(QCA Scheme of Work for ICT, Aims and Purposes)

The 'Communicating' strand for ICT is inextricably linked with developing literacy. Computer access is a great resource for independent, group and class work, and is too valuable a tool to remain unused during the development of literacy skills. It is a great motivator and encourages collaborative work that can become more focused as children's attention is extended.

Within the suggested Year 3 Fiction *Pelican Shared Writing* activities, there are some clear links with units from the QCA Scheme of Work for ICT, particularly:

- Unit 3A (Combining Text and Graphics)
- Unit 4A (Writing for Different Audiences)

Links to the most relevant National Curriculum Programme of Study for ICT are listed in the table opposite.

The differentiated writing frames for Year 3 (Fiction and Non-Fiction) are available on the CD-ROM entitled *Pelican Shared Writing Year 3* (ISBN 0582 50986 6), which can be easily installed on any machine supporting Microsoft Word. Here they may be adapted, should you so wish, to suit your particular needs. The CD-ROM also provides cross-referencing charts for both Writing and ICT targets, including the ICT Programme of Study references and links to the QCA Scheme of Work for ICT – collated and readily available for inclusion in planning records.

Year 3 Fiction
Relevant objectives from the ICT Programme of Study

Pupils should be taught:

1a
to talk about what information they need and how they can find and use it *[for example, searching the internet or a CD-ROM, using printed material, asking people]*

1b
how to prepare information for development using ICT, including selecting suitable sources, finding information, classifying it and checking it for accuracy *[for example, finding information from books or newspapers, creating a class database, classifying by characteristics and purposes, checking the spelling of names is consistent]*

2a
how to develop and refine ideas by bringing together, organising and reorganising text, tables, images and sound as appropriate *[for example, desktop publishing, multimedia presentations]*

3a
how to share and exchange information in a variety of forms, including e-mail *[for example, displays, posters, animations, musical compositions]*

3b
to be sensitive to the needs of the audience and think carefully about the content and quality when communicating information *[for example, work for presentation to other pupils, writing for parents, publishing on the internet]*

4a
review what they and others have done to help them develop their ideas

4b
describe and talk about the effectiveness of their work with ICT, comparing it with other methods and considering the effect it has on others *[for example, the impact made by a desktop-published newsletter or poster]*

National Curriculum for England, ICT Programmes of Study

Term 1 Unit of work 1:

Write descriptions based on models

Resource Book pages 2–5

Writing objective:
T11: To develop the use of settings in own stories
Links to sentence/word level work
S11: To demarcate the end of a sentence with a full stop.

Text Copymasters: C8–11

Discussing the Text

- Read 'An Autumn Wood' together.
- Using the acetate sheet, highlight the words and phrases which provide answers to the following questions: *What time of day is it? What is the weather like? Apart from the title, what tells us it is autumn? What is the writer comparing trees to?* (people crying)
- Read 'The Castle' together.
- Discuss who "He" might be e.g. a knight returning home from a long journey. Highlight the words and phrases which provide answers to the following questions: *How do we know that the person is pleased ? What time of day is it? What is the weather like? What is the writer comparing the castle to?* (An old person) *Is it a friendly old person? How do we know?* (winked, welcome)
- Read 'A Grey Day' together.
- Highlight the words and phrases which provide answers to the following questions: *What time of day is it? What is the weather like? What season is it? Where and why does the writer use alliteration? Where and why does the writer use repetition?*
- Read 'City Spring' together.
- Highlight the words and phrases which provide answers to the following questions: *What time of day is it? What is the weather like? Other than the word spring, what tells us which season it is?* Discuss the use of one very long sentence followed by a one-word sentence

Shared Writing

Session 1
Teacher demonstration

- Turn back to 'An Autumn Wood'. Tell the children that you are going to write a description of the same setting but change it to a snowy winter morning (see Shared Writing Example opposite). Choose a title e.g. 'A Winter Wood'.
- As you write, draw attention to the sentence construction e.g. *I need to start with the time of day so I'm going to write 'Morning' and a comma. Now I want to use the same pattern of three adjectives describing the smell so I'm going to write: 'the sharp, crisp and frosty smell of Winter was in the air'. Now I need a full stop.* Complete the description.

Teacher scribing

- Turn to 'The Castle'. Tell the children that you are going to write a description of the same setting but change it to a rainy evening. *Shall we have heavy stormy rain or just a light shower?* (See Shared Writing Example opposite.)
- Underline the parts of the description which will need to be changed

e.g. 'stretching up towards a cloudless sky.' Invite and discuss suggested changes. (Children can write their suggestions on whiteboards, working in pairs.) Either annotate the passage or rewrite completely.

Shared Writing Example:

A Winter Wood Morning, and the sharp, crisp and frosty smell of Winter was in the air. The snow lay thinly on the branches as if the trees themselves were wrapped in winter overcoats. Trees were keeping warm with snow just as soon they would be warmed by the sunshine of Spring.

The Castle He stopped. There was the castle in front of him with its walls and towers stretching up to a grey and darkening sky. He smiled. It seemed like the castle was reaching up to the gentle rain ... trying to wash the dust from its old granite bones. Lights in the windows beckoned him and the wet, shiny drawbridge was down to welcome him home.

Session 2
Supported composition

- Re-read 'A Grey Day'. Tell children that they are going to write a description of the same setting, but change it to a hot summer day. They should use three sentences which, like the model, describe the weather, who and what can be seen on the beach and the colour of the sky and sea.
- Ask for suggestions for a title. Discuss the first sentence and what will have to change. Discuss whether or not to use a question as in the model.
- Children should work in pairs using whiteboards to write the first sentence e.g. 'The beach was full now for everyone wanted to enjoy the hot sun, cooling breeze and gentle waves.'
- Ask pairs to check each other's compositions for effectiveness and to make sure they do describe the weather. Discuss some of the children's sentences and, perhaps, write up some of the best.
- Repeat with the next two sentences.

Independent Writing

- Re-read 'City Spring' with the class. Tell the children that they are going to write a description of the same setting, but make the time of year the middle of December. Discuss how this would change the description and take suggestions for a title e.g. Christmas in the City. Children should then write their own descriptions.
- Write a description of a playground on a foggy day or a funfair at night.
- Complete the Describing settings grid (Copymaster C1). Choose one to write about.

Checking Children's Learning

- *Why do we need to describe the settings in our stories?*
- *Should we use long sentences, short sentences or a mixture?*
- *What do we need at the ends of sentences?*

Revisiting the Objective

- Write a description based on 'City Spring' for November 5th.
- Complete the Describing settings grid (Copymaster C1) as a shared writing activity.

Term 1 Unit of work 2:

Complete the dialogue

Resource Book pages 6–7

Writing objective:
T10: Using reading as a model, to write own passages of dialogue
Links to sentence/word level work
W19: common vocabulary for introducing and concluding dialogue

Text Copymasters: C12–13

Discussing the Text

- Read the character descriptions of Mr Simpkins, Marcus and Kerry with the class.
- *What kind of relationship might the two children have with their next door neighbour?* List the children's suggestions e.g. They could be friends. The children could help him. They don't speak because the old man doesn't like children.
- Read 'The Conversation'. *What does this tell us about the relationship between the characters?* Which of the children's predictions now seem the more likely?
- *What does this conversation tell us about the way we should write speech or dialogue?* Draw out and perhaps list: speech marks, use of capital letters, starting speech on a new line, punctuation before the closing speech marks, showing who is speaking. When talking about speech marks, ask children to help you underline the actual speeches in one colour and reporting clauses e.g. 'whispered Marcus' in another.

Shared Writing

Teacher demonstration

- Tell the children that Marcus and Kerry have been learning about helping people in school and they have decided to try and help their neighbour. Give children a minute talking in pairs to think of what sorts of help they could offer him.
- Explain that you are going to continue the dialogue and you need to write a linking sentence or two (see Shared Writing Example opposite). Compose orally before you write.
- Continue with the first part of the conversation, including a commentary on writing direct speech e.g. *I'm going to have Mr Simpkins saying 'What do you two want?' so I need to start with the speech marks to show he is talking. This is how we write them. Now I need a capital letter to start my sentence.* Write the sentence. (*He's asking a question so what do I need here? Yes, a question mark.*) But do not put in the closing speech marks. *I put speech marks at the beginning to show he was talking, now I need to put them in at the end to show that he has finished speaking. Now I'm going to write 'Mr Simpkins asked' to show who is speaking and I'm going to add 'crossly' to show how he was feeling.*
- Write the next part of the dialogue as in the Shared Writing Example, commentating as you go.

Teacher scribing

- Scribe the children's suggestions as to what help Kerry and Marcus might say they can offer (see Shared Writing Example opposite).
- Ask the children to help you turn the first one into a sentence e.g. '"We could take your dog for a walk for you," said Marcus.' *How do I need to start?* etc.
- Discuss what Mr Simpkins might say in refusing the offer. Write his reply.

Supported Composition

- Write the next sentence(s) containing Kerry's suggestion for help.
- Check and compare.
- Write Mr Simpkins' refusal then check and compare the sentences.

Shared Writing Example:

The children heard a dog barking as they waited anxiously.
Eventually the door opened.
"What do you two want?" Mr Simpkins asked crossly.
"We thought we would come round and see if there was anything we could do to help you," replied Marcus.
"We really would like to help you if we could," Kerry added.
" What could you do?" asked Mr Simpkins

Suggestions for helping Mr Simpkins

- walk the dog
- fetch library books
- do some sweeping or weeding in the garden
- come in for a chat

Independent Writing

- Complete the conversation with Mr Simpkins refusing the first three offers of help saying he can manage. He accepts the final one of coming in for a chat because he is lonely.
- Write the conversation between Kerry, Marcus and Mum when they tell her about their visit next door.

Checking Children's Learning

- Can children write and place speech marks appropriately? (Don't allow the exaggeration of '66 and 99' when children write inverted commas!)
- Can they list the points they need to remember when writing dialogue? (speech marks, use of capital letters, starting speech on a new line, punctuation before the closing speech marks, showing who is speaking.)

Revisiting the Objective

- Write a telephone conversation between Mr Simpkins and his daughter in which he tells her about Marcus and Kerry's visit.

Term 1 Unit of work 3:

Write imaginative comparisons

Resource Book pages 8–10

Writing objective:
T13: To write imaginative comparisons.

Text Copymasters: C14–16

Discussing the Text

- Read the first two extracts from poems with the children.
- These poets are both comparing one thing to something else. *What two things is Grace Nichols comparing an elephant to? Why is this more effective than simply saying that an elephant is very big?*
- Read the next extract and discuss how the poet makes his point by exaggeration and by comparing the coat to something that was big enough to contain a football crowd.
- Read the next three prose extracts together. Ask children to identify how each author creates a vivid picture of the character (by making a comparison to something else). You may wish to introduce the term simile.
- *Which writers use exaggeration to create an effect? Which writers compare one thing to something else? Why do they do this?*

Shared Writing

Session 1
Teacher demonstration

- Tell children you are going to write a poem using imaginative comparisons which will give readers a picture of the size and nature of an elephant and that you will do the first line for them.
- Write the frame for the poem as in the Shared Writing Example opposite or have it already written.
- Complete the first line e.g. *African elephants have got very big ears which flap about so I'm going to write 'Ears like sails in the wind'*

Teacher scribing

- Ask children for suggestions as to what an elephant's legs can be compared to. Discuss their suggestions and write one.
- Remind children that Grace Nichols compared the elephant's feet to giant paperweights and ask them to write other ideas on their whiteboards. Discuss their suggestions and write one.

Supported composition

- Children complete the remaining lines, individually or in pairs.
- Discuss some of the children's choices and select examples to complete the poem.
- Read the finished poem all together.

Session 2
Teacher demonstration

- Re-read Betsy Byars' description. Tell children you are going to write another description of a fox – an urban fox standing under a lamp-post (see Shared Writing Example opposite).

- *I need an introductory sentence so I'm going to write 'The fox stood under the light and I could see him clearly.' Let's read that back ... I'm not really happy with that so I'm going to change it to make it sound better.* Change the sentence to the one in the Shared Writing Example, explaining what you are doing.
- Continue the description as in the Shared Writing Example below. Explain why you have used certain images e.g. *A fox has a reddish brown coat so I'm going to write ... Foxes are always on the lookout for danger so I'm going to say that he has his nose in the air ... Why do you think I've chosen to write 'the red smell of danger'? Can a smell really have a colour?*

Teacher scribing

- Tell the children you are going to write a similar description together, this time of a cat at night.
- Brainstorm and list suggestions for the cat's appearance – coat, tail, whiskers, ears – and things you could compare them to e.g. ears like little black triangles, fur which looked like a piece of the night sky.
- Take suggestions for first composing an introductory sentence and then one describing the cat's coat. Discuss and select examples of each.

Supported composition

- Children complete the remaining sentences, individually or in pairs.
- Discuss some of the suggestions and select examples to complete the description. Read the finished description all together.

Shared Writing Examples:

Elephant

Ears like *sails in the wind*
Legs like *tall tree trunks*
Feet like *heavy circles*
Eyes like *wise little windows*
Trunk like *a friendly snake*
Tusks like *ivory swords*
Body like *a comfy cushion*
Elephant: a huge but gentle grey giant.

Fox

As the fox stood in the pool of light, I could see him clearly. His eyes shone like amber stones and his coat was the colour of treacle toffee. His nose was raised, ready for the red smell of danger.

Independent Writing

- Children write their own elephant poem using the same structure.
- Write a prose description of an animal children have seen in the zoo.

Checking Children's Learning

- *Why do writers sometimes compare one thing to another?*

Revisiting the Objective

- Write additional lines for Roger McGough's poem e.g. *as quiet as a mouse, as loud as a trumpet, as big as a house.*

Term 1 Unit of work 4:

Change the story into a playscript

Resource Book pages 11–13

Writing objective:
T15: To write simple playscripts based on own reading
Links to sentence/word level work
S11: To write in complete sentences

Text Copymasters: C17–19

Discussing the Text

- *Why is David whining and complaining?*
- *Does this story remind you of any journeys you have been on?*
- Using the acetate, ask the children to help you underline all the examples of where someone is actually speaking.
- Use a different colour to underline all the instances of reported speech e.g. 'Mum told the children to be quiet …'

Shared Writing

Session 1
Teacher demonstration

- Tell the children that you are going to turn this short story into a play.
- *All plays have a cast list – a list of people in the play and who they are.* Write 'Cast list'. *Who are the people in the story?* List the names vertically. *Now I need to say who they are. Mum and Dad are obvious but Megan and David could be anyone so I'm going to write …* (See Shared Writing Example.)
- *The next thing we need is to say where the first part of our play is taking place. We call this the Scene so I'm going to write Scene 1. The family are in their car and I think they are somewhere on the motorway so that is what I'm going to write.*
- *Now we can start to write what the cast or characters are saying.* Refer to the underlining in the story and ask the children who speaks first and to read out the first words that are spoken.
- *When we are writing a play we put the name of the person who is speaking on the left of the page. I'm going to write David in capital letters. Now I'm going to leave a space and write down what he says.* Point out that we do not use speech marks or 'said' in playscripts.
- *Who speaks next? Yes, Megan … wait a minute, is it important that we know it's the tenth time David has asked that question? I think it is so I am going to introduce another character called the Narrator. The Narrator is the name we give to the person who tells the story in between some of the characters' speeches.* Add the Narrator to the cast list and write his/her speech as in the example, using a full stop at the end.
- Write MEGAN. Ask children to read the underlined words in the story that Megan says for you to write them down.
- *I need to show that Megan gives her brother a shove here. I could have the Narrator telling us but I'm going to have something called a stage direction instead. Stage directions tell characters what to do. This is how I'm going to write the stage direction …* (See Shared Writing Example opposite.)

- Pause at this point to read aloud what you have written so far. Read the Narrator's speech as an exclamation: *I think I need something stronger than a full stop here so I'm going to change it to an exclamation mark. That gives a clue as to how to say this speech.*
- Identify the next speaker in the story (Dad) and what he says. *How does he say it? I'm going to show that he is sighing as another stage direction before the words he speaks like this …* (See Shared Writing Example below.)

Teacher scribing

- *Let's read our next bit of underlining … So which character is going to speak next? Yes, it's Mum* (write MUM) *but we've got to write down what she actually said; what could we write?* Discuss the children's suggestions, select and scribe one.
- Repeat as above with Megan's reply.

Shared Writing Example:

Cast list:	Mum; Dad; Megan – their daughter; David – her younger brother
Scene 1:	The family are in a car somewhere on the motorway.
DAVID	Dad, are we nearly there yet?
NARRATOR	That was the tenth time that David had asked that question!
MEGAN	I'm getting fed up with you!
	(Megan gives her brother a shove.)
DAD	*(sighing)* Look it's bad enough driving for two hours without having to listen to you two arguing.
MUM	Yes, be quiet the pair of you! Can't you find something to do?
MEGAN	No. I've finished reading my comics AND I've done all the puzzles in my book.

Session 2
Supported composition

- It is suggested that the whole session is devoted to supported writing. Read what you have written so far with the children and recap on the features of playscript writing which were taught in the previous session.
- Continue changing the story into the playscript – one or two speeches at a time. Ask/remind the children frequently about the conventions and features of playscript writing. Scene 2 should be the final paragraph of the story.

Independent Writing

- Complete the text transformation if this has not been finished.
- Continue Scene 2.

Checking Children's Learning

- Have the children laid out their scripts appropriately?
- Can they define the functions of: a cast list, narrator, stage directions etc?

Revisiting the Objective

- Add another scene where the family get lost on the journey to the sea.

Term 1 Unit of work 5:

Revise a piece of writing

Resource Book pages 11–13

This unit does not address a specific writing composition objective. It focuses instead on the crucial skill of revising writing, which is an ongoing part of teaching writing.

Text Copymasters: C17–19

Discussing the Text

- Mask Resource Book page 10 with a blank sheet of paper held by clips or Blu-tack.
- Re-read page 11 together and tell children that you are going to do something different with it.

Shared Writing

Teacher demonstration

- Tell children the following: *Wendy Body wrote this story with a very particular purpose. It had to be something which we could turn into a playscript very easily so she put in lots of speech. She didn't write much in the way of details or descriptions which might have made it even more interesting. So today that's what we are going to do. We are going to revise Wendy Body's writing and see if we can improve it.*
- Clip the acetate over the page. *We'll mark the things we think we should change first of all and then we'll do the writing. Let's look at the opening … Do you think we could improve it? … Yes, I think we need to add something here so I'm going to write '1. Expand the opening'.* Annotate as in the Shared Writing Example opposite then read the first two sentences. *I think we should say something about David – perhaps that he is Megan's younger brother – but for now I'll just mark it like this* (number 2 on the Shared Writing Example).
- Go through the rest of the page marking where you and the children think changes could be made (see Shared Writing Example and ensure you mark number 4). Anything requiring more than a single word or two of immediate change should be numbered and left.

Teacher scribing

- *Let's look at what we could do to the opening of the story to improve it. Openings often introduce the setting and say something about the characters.* Take suggestions from the children. Compose sentences orally and then write them on the facing sheet of paper (see Shared Writing Example). Will you still need 'Megan' in the actual text or can it be crossed out and 'She' substituted?
- Have you said anything about David in the opening? If you have, cross out the annotated number 2. If not, tell children that you could insert some detail here and discuss possibilities before writing e.g. 'Freckle-faced David, Megan's younger brother'.
- Continue with any necessary revision until you get to number 4 on the example.

Supported composition

- Number 4 on the example: *I think we should say how Dad is feeling here and why he is feeling like that.* Ask children to quickly list words to describe his feelings and why e.g. hot – car is hot, cross – children quarrelling, tired – long drive. Select and discuss alternatives.

Shared Writing Example:

1 *Expand the opening*

I Spy ...

2 *age? appearance?*

Megan was bored. David was even more bored. "Dad, are we nearly there yet?" he whined.

3 *long journey?*

This was the tenth time that David had asked the same question.

"I'm getting *really* **fed up with you! said Megan** *crossly***, giving her brother a ~~shove.~~** *dig in the ribs?*

Dad sighed and then said, "Look, it's bad enough driving for two hours, without having to listen to you two arguing." 4 *how dad's feeling*

Mum told the children to be quiet and find something to do. Megan replied that not only had she finished reading her comics but she had also done all the puzzles in her book. 5 *How? Do we need to say?*

1. The Griffiths family were on their way to the seaside. Everyone was looking forward to their holiday but it felt as if the journey would never be over. They had been driving along the motorway for nearly two hours. Red-haired Megan was chewing her plaits. She was bored.

4. Dad was starting to feel tired because he had been driving for a long while and it was hot in the car. Mum wanted him to concentrate on his driving so she told the children to be quiet and find something to do.

- Choose one and ask children to compose a sentence to insert in the text. Select and discuss alternatives before choosing one to write on your sheet.
- *Does this new sentence make us want to change the next one at all?* If so, ask for suggestions (see Shared Writing Example).

Independent Writing

- In pairs, using Copymasters C17–19, children should annotate the rest of the text marking where they think changes should or could be made. Independently (or in pairs for less able children) they should use their notes to rewrite any new passages. They can then do a cut and paste using the copymaster and the new passages to create a new version of the story.

Checking Children's Learning

- Discuss what children have changed in their versions and why.

Term 1 Unit of work 6:

Write shape poems

Resource Book pages 14–16

Writing objective:
T14: To invent … a range of shape poems
Links to sentence/word level work:
S13: To use commas to separate items in a list

Text Copymasters: C20–23

Discussing the Text

- Read the poem 'Sleeping' together.
- Draw attention to/ask the children to identify the examples of alliteration.
- Point out that this shape poem has been illustrated but that shape poems quite often stand alone without illustration because their shape suggests the picture.
- Read 'Lamp-post' together. (Wendy Body really does have a dog named Merlin who has a brother called Muffin.)
- How is this poem different from the previous one? (No rhyme or alliteration.)

Shared Writing

Teacher demonstration

- Have the resource book open at page 16 with acetate clipped in place and a sheet of paper clipped to the facing page to mask it.
- Tell the children you are going to write a shape poem in the frame and you want to make it a rhyming poem.
- On the facing sheet of paper, write the word 'sliding': *I want to use this word – can you think of any words which rhyme with it?* Make sure you get 'hiding' and 'gliding'.
- Model Writing Example 1: *Snakes are very smooth so I'm going to start by saying 'Smooth and sliding'* ... Look at rhyming words … *I think I'll use 'hiding' but snakes don't hide all the time so I'll write 'sometimes hiding'. Now I'll add two other things that snakes do: 'sleeping, eating' and I'll finish off by using another rhyming word 'gliding' … No, I'll change that to 'dangerously gliding' because it sounds better and says something else about snakes.*
- Read aloud what you have written. If you have already taught the use of commas in lists, ask the children to identify the missing punctuation. If not, identify the missing punctuation yourself and explain why the commas are needed. Re-read the poem together.

Teacher scribing

- Swap the acetate and paper over and tell children that you are going to write a non-rhyming shape poem about a Christmas tree together.
- Tell children that the first 'section' of the tree poem is about before it is decorated and the second about its decorations. This can be continued in the third part, finishing up with children around the tree.
- Ask for word and phrase suggestions and write them on the facing sheet of paper. *I'll start us off … 1. tall and green … 2. … silently waits.* Encourage a mix of long and short phrases similar to those in the Shared Writing Example opposite.

Supported composition

- Write 'Tall / and green,' at the top of the tree shape … *'silently waits' doesn't make sense by itself so we need to write 'it silently waits'. What is the tree waiting for? Yes, to be decorated, so we'll write that.*
- Read the word and phrase suggestions together. Ask children to list them on their whiteboards in what they think would be a good order for the poem.
- Discuss choices, make selections and write the rest of the poem.

Shared Writing Examples:

Snake

1. Smooth and sliding, sometimes hiding, sleeping, eating, ~~gliding~~ dangerously gliding.
2. ~~Twisting~~ Slow curves of smooth dry scales sliding through the grass – ~~looking~~ searching for somewhere to ~~hide~~ sleep.

Christmas tree

NB: Suggested line breaks will depend on your handwriting size!

Tall / and green / it silently waits / to be decorated with a / silver star, / twists of tinsel, / shining golden baubles,/ and brightly coloured /lights which will flicker /on and off / reflecting / the happiness on/ the children's faces/ as they stand smiling/ around/ the/ tree.

Independent Writing

- Children use copymaster versions of either the snake or the tree shape (Copymaster C22 or C23) to write their own poems. The task can be made more challenging by asking the more able children to use alliteration or rhyme.
- Write a shape poem on one of these topics or choose another. *You can sketch an outline shape for the first draft but the finished version should be without a shape framing it.*

Checking Children's Learning

- Do children understand that the shape of shape poems reflects what the poem is about? Is this evident in their work?
- *What does alliteration mean?*
- Ask children to find other examples of shape poems in anthologies.

Revisiting the Objective

- Use Example 2 of the snake poem above. Draft it for the children and then involve them in making it more alliterative as per the changes in the example.

Term 1 Unit of work 7:

Write examples of openings and endings

Resource Book pages 18–21

Writing objective:
T12: To investigate … story openings and endings

Text Copymasters: C24–27

Session 1

Discussing the Text

- Introduce and read all the story openings.
- Tell children that openings to stories introduce characters and settings and, importantly, aim to "grab" the reader, make them want to read on.
- *Which openings introduce characters? Which openings introduce settings? Which introduce both? Do they all make you want to read on? Do the openings give us clues as to what kind of stories they might be introducing? Can you tell which stories might be for younger readers and which ones might be for older readers? What makes you think that?*

Shared Writing

Teacher demonstration

- Tell children that you are going to make all these openings introduce both settings and characters. *Some do it already, so which ones will we need to work on?*
- *I'm going to start with the second one on page 19 by Martin Waddell which has got a character and not a setting.* Read the opening to the children: 'Tom Murphy was young when his father was hung.' *I want to write something which tells us about the setting but I'm wondering if it would spoil this sentence if I added to it and made it longer. Or could I add something which kept the rhythm of the sentence? I want to add 'many years ago in Ireland'. I could either put it at the beginning or at the end.*
- *Let's see how they both sound … 'Many years ago in Ireland, Tom Murphy was young when his father was hung.' Or I could say, 'Tom Murphy was young when his father was hung – many years ago in Ireland.' Which do you think sounds better?*
- *I think putting it at the end keeps the rhythm of the sentence better so I'm going to write that one.* Write the sentence, commentating on the punctuation choice. Read it all together.

Teacher scribing

- Read the first Martin Waddell opening: 'One day, a duck tried on an egg-shell as a hat.' *We could introduce the setting by adding, 'One day, in the corner of a sunny farmyard, a duck tried on an egg-shell as a hat.' Or, 'One day, on the banks of the village pond, a duck tried on an egg-shell as a hat.' Could it take place anywhere else?*
- Ask children to write a sentence on their whiteboards.
- Discuss the children's suggestions and write one. Read it all together.

Supported composition

- Read the opening, 'It was a stormy night with clouds that growled their way across the thundery sky.' Discuss who a main character might be and list children's suggestions e.g. a lost boy, a weary traveller.
- Ask children to select a character, compose a sentence orally in pairs and then write it down on their whiteboards.
- Discuss their choices.

Sessions 2 and 3

Discussing the Text

- Introduce and read all the story endings.
- Which ones do children think work really well? Why?
- Give out copies of Copymaster C2 to each pair. Go through it and explain that these are some different ways of ending stories.
- Ask children to note down which ending in the Resource Book fits which type. *The first type says something about the way the character feels … Which of the endings is like that? Yes, the one about Tinker, so write 'Tinker ending' under the first heading.*
- Ask children to complete the sheet (see Shared Writing Example). Discuss what they have done and reinforce the idea, as with the Tinker passage, that endings can be of more than one type.

Shared Writing Example: What kind of ending is it?

- **Says something about the way the character feels:**
  Tinker ending
  They were too tired to think about all that had happened so they went home and went to bed.
- **Adds some descriptive details about the setting:**
  Robin ending
  So they went home and slowly climbed the stairs to their bedroom. They were really pleased to be back in their safe and welcoming house once more.
- **Says that the character has changed or learned something:**
  Tinker ending
  Tired out, they went home and went to bed. They knew that when they woke up in the morning they need never be afraid of spiders again.
- **The author 'speaks' to the reader directly:**
  Hare and Tortoise ending.
  So they went home and went to bed … I expect you would have done the same if you'd had an adventure like that!
- **Says something about the future:**
  The little pig ending.
  For now, they went home and went to bed but they knew that the giant spiders might return again.
- **Ends with a question:**
  Ranjit ending
  Wearily they went home to go to bed, wondering … Could they ever see spiders in quite the same way again?

Shared Writing

Teacher demonstration

- Tell the children that you are going to do some work on story endings. Point out that sometimes story endings are not very good like the examples you are going to show them.
- Write the following: 'I woke up to find it had all been a dream.' *This isn't very interesting is it, so I'm going to see if I can improve it. I'm going to write 'I opened my eyes and realised that I had been dreaming. There was no need for me to feel scared any more.' While I write it, see if you can decide what type of ending it is.*
- Discuss the children's views and ask their opinions on whether or not it IS a better ending.

Teacher scribing

- *I'm going to write an ending to a story about some children who have had an adventure with giant spiders.* Write the following: 'So they went home and went to bed.' *But it's not a very interesting ending, is it? Let's see if we can improve it. Look at your sheets and remind yourselves about the different types of endings.*
- Take the first type of ending and ask for suggestions as to how the sentence could be changed or added to in that way. Discuss the suggestions and select one to write as a model or use the example.
- Repeat with each of the different types of ending.
- Read and review the list of alternative endings.

Supported composition

- Read the above list again if it is a new session. Tell children that they are going to do the same thing again but using a different sentence. *This time the story is about some children who have been kidnapped and then saved. This is the ending you are going to work on: 'So they went home and had their tea.'* Write the sentence.
- *How can we change or add to this ending so that it says something about the way the characters feel? Discuss it with your partner for a few seconds and then be ready to give me your suggestions.*
- Take a few suggestions and discuss which one to write.
- *Now how can we change or add to the ending so that it says something about the setting?* Children write the sentence(s) on their whiteboards. Give a couple of examples first if you feel they need it.
- Repeat with some/all of the different types of ending.
- Ask individual children to read out their work and discuss their efforts.

Independent Writing

- Continue with the above activity if it has not been completed.

Openings:

- Ask the children to write an opening for the story of Goldilocks and the Three Bears. Decide if it will introduce Goldilocks or the bears and what can be said about the setting.
- *Look back through stories you have written and find one where you can work on the opening. See if you can improve it by trying to add details about the character or setting. Can you write it so it really grabs your readers and makes them want to read on?*

Endings:

- Try writing two or three different types of ending for the story of Cinderella – or another story which is well known to the children.
- *Look back through stories you have written and find one where you can work on the ending. See if you can improve it by trying one of the different types of ending that we've been working on.*

Checking Children's Learning

- Can the children describe what makes a successful opening?
- How successful have they been at rewriting their own story opening?
- How many different types of ending can the children recall?
- How successful are they at changing one type of ending to another?

Revisiting the Objective

- Write some 'Advice on openings and endings' posters to display in the classroom. Brainstorm ideas and examples to go in bullet points under the headings of *Good openings …* and *Good Endings …*
- Use examples of openings and endings from children's work to revise with the whole class.
- Use Supported composition to write an opening and ending for a story the class already know e.g. Little Red Riding Hood.

Term 1 Unit of work 8:

Write a story in paragraphs

Resource Book pages 22–25

Writing objective:
T16: To begin to organise stories into paragraphs
Links to sentence/word level work
S7: The basic conventions of speech punctuation

Text Copymasters: C28–31

Discussing the Text

- Introduce the text by explaining that it is a story plan which sets out what should go in each paragraph. Tell children that you are going to use this story plan to make a class book or wall story.
- Remind children what a paragraph is i.e. a section or chunk of text which usually contains one main idea. Paragraphs are there to make a text easier to read and understand. New paragraphs signal new ideas or events, a change in time or place and, sometimes, a new speaker in a passage of dialogue. In print, paragraphs are marked by leaving one line's space in between each paragraph. We do this in handwriting as well. However, you can also leave a space at the start of the first line.
- Read the story outline with the children.
- Discuss the segmentation in the outline and see if children agree with it. Some paragraphs, e.g. number 10, could be split into two paragraphs if more was to be made of the walk home – stopping at the shops, for example.

Shared Writing

Teacher demonstration

- Discuss whether the two children are boys or girls and what they and the dog will be called.
- Write the first paragraph (see Shared Writing Example below) commentating as you go, e.g. *I'm going to start with "Child" speaking so I need to put in the speech marks ... 'through' is a tricky word, can anyone remember how to spell it? ... It might not be safe to have the children in the woods all alone so I'm going to say that the children can see Mum from where they are.*
- Read the paragraph all together.

Shared Writing Example:

"*Dog*, where are you?" called *Child*. He/she smiled as the dog came running through the trees. It was a warm sunny afternoon and *Child* and *Child* were out with their dog, *Name*. They were walking through the edge of the little wood close to where they lived. The wood was so close to their house that the children could see their mum in the garden.

Teacher scribing

- *Now we're going to write the second paragraph. I shall leave a space to show that it is a new paragraph. and start it off. Write: 'Child* and *Child plus Surname* were brother and sister/brothers/sisters.'
- Discuss what needs to go in this paragraph about their appearances, age etc. and reach consensus.
- Give children 30 seconds or so to compose sentences in pairs. Take two or three examples, amend as necessary and then scribe one sentence at a time.

Supported composition

- Children write an opening sentence for paragraph three. This introduces the fact that the characters are walking along and having a conversation about school. Discuss some of the sentences and choose one to write.
- Ask for ideas on what the characters might be saying to each other e.g. telling the other about a model one of them has made, asking the other if he/she had seen the fight in the playground that the one had watched.
- Remind the children about how direct speech is written and laid out.
- Sentence by sentence, discuss some of the children's efforts, make a selection and then scribe.
- Continue with paragraph four.

Independent Writing

- Designated groups write paragraphs for certain sections of the story. The amount will be ability related: least able children can do one paragraph, the most able can complete the story.
- Split the children into groups to revise, edit and illustrate the class book.
- Try writing a story outline in paragraphs as in the model.

Checking Children's Learning

- *What is a paragraph?*
- *When do we need to start a new paragraph?*
- *How do we set out paragraphs in writing?*

Revisiting the Objective

- Write a similar story outline in paragraphs adapting the text from the Resource Book:
  - two children are out walking with their dog
  - the dog finds a purse buried under some leaves
  - the children debate what to do and decide to go to the police station with their mum
  - they hand the purse in
  - on the way home the dog finds something else under a hedge – a baby's shoe?
- Use Teacher scribing and Supported composition to write part of the story. Children can then complete it independently.

Term 2 Unit of work 9:

Describe and sequence key incidents

Resource Book pages 26–29

Writing objective:

T7: To describe and sequence key incidents in a variety of ways

Links to sentence/word level work

S6 & **S7**: The use of commas

Text Copymasters: C32–33

Discussing the Text

- Introduce 'Ant and Grasshopper' saying that it is one of Aesop's fables which has been rewritten by Geraldine McCaughrean. Remind them that fables set out to teach a lesson and they always have a moral.
- Read the story aloud. *How would you describe each of the characters? How do you think both characters feel at the end of the story?* Discuss the implication of the last sentence – will Ant regret his refusal to help? *What is Aesop trying to teach us in this story?*
- Ask children to identify the author's use of imaginative comparisons on Resource Book page 28 and discuss the effectiveness of the images.
- Identify and discuss where the commas occur and how they help the reader.

Shared Writing

Teacher demonstration

- Tell children you are going to list the important things that happened in the story or the key incidents. Say that they do not have to be in order. *I'm going to start off by saying: Winter and Grasshopper has no food … Notice that I don't need to write this in a complete sentence. I only need to write enough to remind me.*
- Ask children to tell you other key incidents (see Shared Writing Example below). Make sure you list them randomly and in a similar form to the example.
- Read the list and ask children to tell you the order in which the incidents happened. Number the first two accordingly.

Shared Writing Example:

- Winter and Grasshopper has nothing to eat
- Ant refuses to help Grasshopper
- Ant tells Grasshopper she should do same
- Grasshopper is too busy enjoying herself to store food
- Goes to Ant and asks for food
- Summer and Ant spends time collecting food

Supported composition

- Give out individual copies of Copymaster C3. Ask children to use the list to sequence the key incidents, writing one statement in each box.
- Compare and check. Point out that this is a way of planning key incidents in a story which could then be used to write it.

Teacher scribing

- Tell children that the key incidents in the story could be represented in another way.
- Draw 2 boxes (vertically or horizontally as in the example below). Head one *Summer* and the other *Winter*.
- Fill in the boxes with the children's help.
- Point out that this kind of planning works best for stories which have two separate times or settings.

Summer	*Winter*
1. Ant collects food	1. Grasshopper has nothing to eat
2. Tells Grasshopper to do same	2. Ant has full larder
3. Grasshopper can't be bothered	3. Asks Ant for food
	4. Ant refuses to help

Independent Writing

- Work in pairs to see if the children can come up with another way of representing the key incidents.
- Use either list of key points to write their own versions of the story. The task can be differentiated by getting the more able children to write the story in flashback, starting with a cold and hungry Grasshopper or the lonely Ant in his larder thinking back to the summer.
- Research another fable from Aesop. List the key incidents in the story in the correct sequence.

Checking Children's Learning

- Can the children explain the point of representing the key incidents in stories? (To show they have understood a story; helpful when it comes to planning stories of their own.)
- Are they able to identify key incidents in a story using "sequential" language e.g. First of all … after that … and then … finally … in the end.

Revisiting the Objective

- Use the 'I Spy' story on page 11 of the Resource Book (Copymaster C17). List the key incidents in the story in the correct sequence. Write a list or make a flow chart. Boxes can correspond with paragraphs.

Term 2 Unit of work 10:

Write alternative sequels

Resource Book pages 26–29

Writing objective:
T10: To write alternative sequels to traditional stories

Text Copymasters: C32–33

Discussing the Text

- Remind the children of the story and re-read the final sentence. Discuss how each character might be feeling.
- Point out that there is not really a very satisfying ending to the story. *What do you think did happen to Grasshopper? I think there are two ways the story could go. Perhaps Grasshopper starved to death during the Winter … . How would Ant have felt about that? Or perhaps Ant changed his mind and shared his food supplies with Grasshopper.*

Shared Writing

Teacher demonstration

- Tell the children that you are going to write another section or sequel to this story and that you have chosen to make Ant help Grasshopper.
- On a sheet of paper write a story plan as in the Shared Writing Example below and discuss it briefly as you write. *Each of these points will be one paragraph.*
- *I'm going to start my writing with Ant thinking about Grasshopper.* Write the first paragraph as in the example. Comment on choice of words, punctuation, using speech to vary things.
- *Now I want to say how Grasshopper is getting on so I'm going to leave Ant for a while and start the next paragraph with 'Meanwhile' … and say where she is. I have to remember to leave a space to show that it is a new paragraph.* Finish the sentence as in the example.

Shared Writing Example:

Story plan:

A few days pass. Ant wonders how Grasshopper is getting on
Grasshopper hidden away, cold and hungry.
Ant feels guilty → goes to look for her
Search
Ant takes Grasshopper back home
Grasshopper says she'll change her ways.

First paragraph:

The cold winter days passed. Sitting in his great, silent larder, Ant used to think about Grasshopper. He wondered how she was getting on with nothing to eat. Was she freezing cold and starving? "Perhaps I was too unkind to her," he thought to himself. "I know she is stupid, but I wouldn't want her to die!"

Meanwhile, Grasshopper was sheltering from the bitter winter wind in the crack of an old stone wall.

Teacher scribing

- *Let's do the next part together. How do you think Grasshopper is feeling?* (How she is feeling herself, i.e. cold and very hungry, regretful; how she feels about Ant.) *Discuss it with your partner for a moment and be ready to give me some suggestions.*
- Take suggestions and discuss briefly – including whether or not you will have her actually speaking to herself or just describe her feelings. Amend or combine suggestions and write the next sentences about her feelings.
- *Can we add anything in the way of descriptive details or imaginative comparisons anywhere?* (e.g. 'the winter wind whistled through her antennae', 'her legs were weak as water')
- *Now let's go back to Ant. I'm going to start a new paragraph and write 'Back in his safe warm home, Ant decided' … What is he going to decide? What shall I write next?*
- Take suggestions and scribe.
- *What could we write next? Write what you think the next sentence could be on your whiteboards and then hold them up so I can choose one.*

Supported composition

- Children write about Ant searching for Grasshopper, finding her and then taking her back to his home. They can work in pairs or individually and should write one or two sentences. These can be discussed before moving on to the next.
- Prompts and reminders to give children:
  – *Think about where Ant might have searched.*
  – *How did he find Grasshopper? Did she see Ant and call out to him?*
  – *What did they say to each other? How did Grasshopper react when Ant said she could go and stay with him for the winter?*

Independent Writing

- Write the final paragraph of the story and try to think of a new moral e.g. Be kind to those in need.
- Write the alternative sequel to the story where Grasshopper dies of hunger.
- Plan an alternative sequel to another story you know well or one that you have written recently.

Checking Children's Learning

- Do children understand the words *alternative* and *sequel*?
- When planning for another story as above, does their planning show that they understand the task? Have they kept the same characters and settings?

Revisiting the Objective

- Repeat the process with an alternative sequel in which Grasshopper is saved because another insect persuades Ant to change his mind.

Term 2 Unit of work 11:

Write an additional verse

Resource Book pages 30–31

Writing objective:

T11: To write new or extended verses for performance

Links to sentence/word level work

S8: Capitalisation … in new lines of poetry

Text Copymaster: C34

Discussing the Text

- Read the poem.
- Identify the rhyming scheme (a, a, b, b, c, c, d, d, e, e). Establish that every line has eight syllables and starts with a capital letter.
- Discuss how the poem could be performed e.g. individuals or groups reading different parts, a group of children quietly repeating *Meow*.

Shared Writing

Session 1

Teacher demonstration

- Use an OHT version of Copymaster C4 or have the following frame handwritten ready to show the children:

My .... of ....
Has seven .... as ....
Who sit ....
And watch ....
....
....
The firelight leaps, the parlour glows,
And, while the music ebbs and flows,
They .... (while ....)
....

- Tell children that you are going to write another verse for the poem using the structure of Mervyn Peake's verse to help you. Remind them of the rhyming scheme and eight syllables to a line.
- *First of all we need the person to write about. I've been thinking about this and I'm going to put Auntie Pat of Potter's Bar … (Potter's Bar is a real place). Mervyn Peake had a one syllable name for the person and a three syllable name for the place and they both start with the same letter. Have I got it right?*
- *Uncle Paul has cats for pets but I'm going to say that Auntie Pat has seven mice … I must remember to start each line with a capital letter even if it isn't a new sentence … as black as … what could I put here? Who can think of something that is black which rhymes with Bar?* Give a clue if necessary.

Teacher scribing

- Continue until the verse is finished. Involve the children where you can, asking them to suggest/complete possible lines or rhyming words e.g. *I think we'll start this line with 'Wearing' … and we need to think of something which rhymes with …* If they get stuck, use the example to guide you.

Shared Writing Example: *With apologies to Mervyn Peake!*

My Auntie Pat of Potter's Bar
Has seven mice as black as tar,
Who sit on her enormous knees
And watch her while they nibble cheese.
As Auntie plays upon her flute,
Wearing a deep-sea diver's suit,
The firelight leaps, the parlour glows,
And, while the music ebbs and flows,
They dance (while joining in the tune)
And shake their whiskers at the moon.

Session 2

Supported composition

- Have children seated in their groups with you standing next to the lowest ability group so that you can support them.
- Recap what was done in the previous session and read out the poem.
- Give out copies of Copymaster C4 to each child. Tell children that they are going to draft another poem using this frame in their groups. Appoint one child to read what the group have composed each time to the class.
- Ask them to discuss, choose and then write names for the first line i.e. Auntie/Uncle/Granny/Grandad/Cousin one syllable name of three syllable place name. *It doesn't have to be a real name, you can invent one. But it must start with the same letter as the person's name.*
- Groups read their first lines.
- *Now discuss and then write the next line. Remember the whole line has to be eight syllables long. If you have problems with the rhyming word at the end, you might have to change your first line. You can use the bottom of the sheet for notes or to try things out.*
- Groups read their next lines.
- Continue until the drafts are complete.

Independent Writing

Work out the best way to read your poem for a class performance.
Write and illustrate fair copies of the group poems for display.
Try writing another verse of your own.

Checking Children's Learning

Can the children tell you the structural features of Mervyn Peake's poem?
How successfully have they applied it in their own writing?

Revisiting the Objective

Repeat the process using another performance poem that the children know.

Term 2 Unit of work 12:

Change characters, settings; plan story

Resource Book pages 32–35

Writing objective:

T9: To write a story plan for own … traditional tale, using story theme from reading but substituting different characters or changing the setting

Text Copymasters: C35–36

Discussing the Text

- Read and discuss the extract with the children. (It comes from *Cinderella* by Stan Cullimore in *Pelican Big Books* published by Longman.)
- Discuss with the class what happens before this point in the story and what will happen after. (Cinderella has two ugly step-sisters who have gone to the ball at which the prince hopes to find a wife but Cinderella is not allowed to go … *extract* … Cinderella dances with the prince and runs away at midnight leaving her slipper. The prince says he will find and marry the owner of the slipper. The slipper fits no one except Cinderella and so they marry.)

Shared Writing

Teacher demonstration

- Use an OHT version of Copymaster C5 or write the headings as you go.
- Tell children you are going to plan a story based on Cinderella but changing certain things. *The first thing I'm going to change is the title. I'm going to call it Cinderboots. He's the character I'm going to have instead of Cinderella.*
- *Now I need to plan who the characters are going to be. I'll start with Cinderboots and say a little bit about who he is … then instead of the Ugly Sisters, I'm going to have two characters called …* Go through the character list as in the Shared Writing Example.
- *Have you guessed what my story is going to be about?* Briefly outline as in the example.
- List the settings as in the example – you could use local or favourite team connections.

Teacher scribing

- *What can we put under Introduction? Remember we are not going to write the first paragraph, we're just going to say what will be in it.*
- Take suggestions and then scribe (see Shared Writing Example opposite).
- Now we need to plan and make a list of the main events in our story. We've got Cinderboots in the kitchen, so what could happen next?
- Discuss children's selections, select/amend and then scribe.
- Continue to the point where the FA Fairy appears.

Supported composition

- Go through the rest of the story listing the main events. Ask children to write them one at a time on their whiteboards and then discuss before making a selection.

Shared Writing Example: A story plan

Title: *Cinderboots*

Character list:

- Cinderboots: a young servant in Baron Beckham's castle who has to wash the kit and clean all the boots of the Baron's football team
- The Ugly Strikers: Gruesome and Ghastly
- The FA Fairy
- Princess Venable: who needs to find a captain for the King's football team

Settings:

Starts with: Baron Beckham's Castle

Moves to: Knot's Forest (the home of Lady Liverpool)

Moves to: Baron Beckham's Castle

Introduction: Cinderboots is cleaning football boots in the kitchen and has still got all the team shirts to iron.

Main events:

- Gruesome and Ghastly talk about the big match against Lady Liverpool's team and how they will play so well that Princess Venable will choose them to be captain of the King's team.
- They go off to the match and leave Cinderboots wishing that he could play.
- The FA Fairy appears to grant his wish and changes his old clothes to Baron Beckham's team colours, his old slippers to a pair of golden football boots, the cat into a fine horse.
- Cinderboots rides off to the match.
- He finds that one of Baron Beckham's team has not turned up and so he plays instead.
-
-

Ending:

Independent Writing

- Using Copymaster C5, write individual story plans – either for Cinderboots or another story. (See the Singerella example below if you do not need to use this as a shared writing lesson.)
- Write the story of Cinderboots using the plan.

Checking Children's Learning

- How successfully can children adapt one story to plan another? Do they preserve and maintain the essential elements?
- What relation do completed stories bear to the initial planning?

Revisiting the Objective

- Use the story of Cinderella again, but this time make it Singerella who wants to take part in a singing contest to find who will be the singer for Prince Tambourine's new pop group. Possible characters could be Baron Keating and Ugly Sisters Crotchet and Quaver and the DJ Fairy, who gives her silver platform shoes …

Term 2 Unit of work 13:

Write character portraits from pictures

Resource Book pages 36–37

Writing objective:

T8: To write portraits of characters … and present them in a variety of ways

Links to sentence/word level work

S2 & S3: Experimenting with the impact of different adjectives; to use the term adjective appropriately

Text Copymasters: C37–38

Session 1

Discussing the Text

- Discuss the illustration on page 36 of the Resource Book (Copymaster C37). *What do you think is happening? Is there a good character and a bad character? A hero and a villain?*

Shared Writing

Teacher demonstration

- Tell children you are going to label the illustration to help with writing a character description.
- Use the acetate to label the illustration. *I'm going to start with the dwarf. First I'm going to write 'Dwarf – hero' at the side. I think he is brave so I'm going to write two adjectives 'brave and courageous' underneath.*
- *Now I'm going to think about his appearance ... he has little legs which look as if they might be very strong so I'm going to draw a label line and write 'short strong legs'. He's holding a sword with jewels in the handle so I'm going to label that 'jewelled sword'.*

Teacher scribing

- *What other labels should I write for the dwarf? What about his face and clothes?* Take suggestions from the children and scribe.
- Complete the labelling of the dwarf.
- *Now let's think about the dragon. I wrote 'Dwarf – hero' for the dwarf so what should I write for the dragon?* e.g. Dragon – villain, huge and fierce.

Supported composition

- Children compose descriptive labels for the dragon. Break the task up so that you give them the noun e.g. *What can we say about its claws?* and they write the adjectives and noun e.g. gigantic sharp claws. Discuss, scribe and move to the next feature.
- Read all the labels together.

Session 2

Discussing the Text

- Discuss the illustration on page 37 of the Resource Book (Copymaster C38). *What do you think is happening here? Do you think the girl is being told off? Why? What do you think the relationship is between the two characters? Do you think they are mother and daughter, teacher and pupil, or sisters?* Choose one relationship.

Teacher demonstration

- Ask the children for adjectives to describe the way each character looks.
- Show children either an OHT or a hand-written version of Copymaster C6. Tell them you are going to describe each character in note form.
- Point out that the chart has two main sections: the first is for information given in the text/story and illustrations i.e. facts. The second is information that the reader can guess or imagine i.e. opinions. Ask where they think information about the characters' appearance will go.
- Tell children that you are going to start them off by writing two things about each character (see Shared Writing Example). Write one thing the illustrations tell us about the situation (see Shared Writing Example).

Shared Writing Example: Character Notes

Character 1 **Name:**	**Character 2** **Name:**	**Situation and how they feel about each other**
What I know from the text or illustrations: young girl aged about 9 short dark hair	What I know from the text or illustrations: young woman aged about 30 quite smartly dressed	What I know from the text or illustrations: they both look serious
What I can also imagine:	What I can also imagine:	What I can also imagine:

Teacher scribing

- Decide on names for each character. Using the children's suggestions, scribe the contents for top left and centre sections.
- *Can we add anything to the situation that we actually know? No, we can't.*

Supported composition

- In pairs, ask children to write down what they can guess or imagine about the girl. Discuss and scribe. Repeat with the woman.
- *What can you guess or imagine about what has happened between the two and how they are feeling? Discuss and then write it in pairs.*
- Discuss and scribe suggestions then read the completed chart.

Independent Writing

- Children choose either the dwarf or the dragon and write a descriptive paragraph about the character.
- Children complete their own versions of Copymaster C6.

Checking Children's Learning

Can children distinguish between fact and opinion when describing characters? Do they understand what an adjective is?

Revisiting the Objective

Use the labelling or chart to write a description of one character.

Term 2 Unit of work 14:

Write a story plan for a traditional story

Resource Book pages 38–39

Writing objective:
T6: To plan main points as a structure for story writing

Text Copymasters: C39–40

Discussing the Text

- Introduce the task and tell children that you are going to plan a story together.
- Read the story plan headings and explain that you don't have to complete them in the same order.

Shared Writing

Session 1
Teacher demonstration

- *The first thing is to decide what the story could be about. I'm going to leave the characters and the setting for a moment because we might want to change them. We're going to write a fantasy story where the main character has two models, a dwarf and a dragon which come to life when someone is in trouble. This time, they rescue a woman who is sleeping when a fire starts in her house by the river. I'll write it down in note form like this* (see Shared Writing Example).

Teacher scribing

- *Let's go back to the characters and see what we need to add or change.*
- Discuss whether or not each of the characters is needed, names and characteristics, and whether additional characters are necessary. See the example but adapt according to what the children come up with. Suggest that the girl, dwarf and dragon could be based on the characters created in the previous unit.
- Discuss and think about the settings. Read what you have written about the basic plot and ask children what this will mean in terms of the settings (the girl's house and the cottage by the river – probably isolated if no one is to spot a fire.) Tell children that when they are planning stories they can always go back and change or add to this when they've got more of an idea of what is going to happen in the story.
- *Let's think about the opening now. I'll start it off …* (see the example)
  How can we carry on? Do we need to say anything about "Girl's" room?
  We could just say that the dwarf jumps off the bedside table and tells her that Mrs Jones needs help. How could I write that? Take suggestions and scribe.

Session 2
Supported composition

- Recap on what has been done so far. *Now we are going to plan the rest of the story. So, what do you think the next thing to happen will be?*
- Children discuss briefly with their partner and then write what they think happens. Ask for examples, discuss, select and scribe.
- Continue in this way until the story is fully planned.
- Think of how the ending might be written.
- Discuss possible suggestions for a title.

Shared Writing Example:

What the story could be about:

girl has two models – a dwarf and a dragon – which come to life when someone in trouble. They rescue woman who is sleeping when fire starts in house by river.

The Characters

- girl, dwarf – *as the character description in the previous Unit*
- dragon – *as physical description in the previous Unit, but friendly and helpful*
- woman – *Mrs Jones, elderly lady, lives alone in cottage close to river*

Opening

It was midnight and something had just woken *Girl*. She looked across at her two favourite models and saw that it was happening again: the dwarf's eyes were glowing and the dragon was just beginning to move its wings.

Independent Writing

- Use Copymaster C7 to plan another story about the girl, the dwarf and the dragon.
- Write the story. Leave time between planning and writing - children often expend their creative energy in planning and have none left for writing! Point out that plans are only to guide the writing, they can be changed as writing progresses.

Checking Children's Learning

- How successful have the children's attempts at planning been?
- *What did you find was the hardest part in doing the plan?*
- *Would any different or extra headings have been useful?*

Revisiting the Objective

- Plan another story using these characters. For example: a neighbour's dog goes missing and it turns out that there is a gang going around and stealing dogs. They keep them in a barn until they are ready to sell them.

Term 3 Unit of work 15:

Make a detailed plan and write the story

Resource Book pages 40–43

Writing objective:

T13: To write more extended stories based on a plan of incidents and set out in simple chapters

Links to sentence/word level work

S4: To use speech marks and other dialogue punctuation

Text Copymasters: C41–42

Discussing the Text

- Introduce the text and say that it is a plan for a longer story which will be written in chapters.
- Read through the chapter plan and ask for children's reactions.
- Discuss possible endings. For example, the box still contains the jewels and the characters speculate as to why the woman never collected them – did her husband kill her? Or the box is empty so the woman must have succeeded in running away. Or there is a note from her husband saying he has taken the jewels.
- Discuss possible titles.

Shared Writing

Session 1

Teacher demonstration

- Tell the children that the outline for Chapter 1 needs to be added to because it leaves us with some questions e.g. Why have the children gone to the aunt? Who are the children? What are their names? What do they look like? Does the story start with them already at their aunt's or as they arrive there? What is the aunt like? What do the children think of her? What is the house like? Write the questions down and ask if there are any others the children want to add.

Teacher scribing

- Tell the children you are going to write a more detailed plan for Chapter 1. Write the heading 'Characters'. Discuss with the class whether the children are boys or girls and what they would like to call them. List the names one at a time, adding some details from the class about age and appearance. Add the aunt to the list.
- Write the heading 'Setting' and under it, 'a stately home – a huge old house made of bricks, built about 400 years ago, very large grounds and gardens, open to the public 4 days a week'. Ask children if there is anything they want to add.
- Select and write one of the questions from the list not already answered. Ask children what they want you to write. Discuss their suggestions, reach consensus and scribe.

Supported composition

- Continue with the rest of the questions. Children should write their suggestions on whiteboards for discussion, selection and you to scribe.

Session 2
Teacher demonstration

- Go briefly through what was done in the previous session. Tell children you are going to start writing Chapter 1.
- *I'm going to start us off and write the first few sentences.* Write something similar to the Shared Writing Example, explaining that you have decided to start with some speech. Remind children about how to punctuate and set it out. **NB: You will need this piece of writing for the next unit.**

Shared Writing Example:

"Wow, look at that!" xxxx cried. "What a fantastic old house!" They were all excited. It was the end of their journey and now the children had their first sight of the house that was to be their home for the next few weeks. They could see the evening sun shining on the windows and a smiling woman waiting for them on the steps in front of the huge door.

Teacher scribing

- *Read the first paragraph with me. Now I think we need to say something about the children and why they are there in the second paragraph. Look at the plan we made … now what shall I write for the first sentence about why they are there?*
- Take suggestions (e.g. 'Name, name and name had come to stay with their aunt xxx for a few weeks while …') *Now we need to say something about the children. Shall we start with the eldest?*
- Continue with fairly brief descriptions of the children and their aunt.

Supported composition

- Sentence by sentence write the next two or three paragraphs to complete the chapter, getting the children into the house and welcomed by their aunt, having something to eat and going to bed.

Independent Writing

- Give each pair or group one of the remaining chapters to write. First discuss and plan any changes/additions to the chapter. Chapter 6 provides the least support so this is more suitable for the most able writers.

Checking Children's Learning

- Can the children amend chapter outlines where necessary?
- Is there sufficient detail in their writing to make the chapter long enough?

Revisiting the Objective

- Plan in more detail and then write the second chapter.

Term 3 Unit of work 16:

Change a third person account into the first person

Resource Book pages 40–43

Writing objective:
T12: To write a first person account
Links to sentence/word level work
S2: First and third person forms of pronouns

Text Copymasters: C41–42

Discussing the Text

- Read through the chapter plan together.
- Ask children if it is written in the first person (someone telling their own story) or the third person (someone telling a story about someone else).
- *How do you know that?* Establish the function of pronouns in this.

Shared Writing

Teacher demonstration

- First remind children about first and third person pronouns by drawing a chart and going through it:

Pronoun	Singular	Plural
First person	I me my mine myself	we us our ours ourselves
Third person	he she him her his hers himself herself	they them their theirs themselves

- Explain that you are going to change the story outline from the third person to the first person. It will be the first person plural because there are three children in the story, not one.
- Use the acetate and tell children that you will do the first chapter outline for them and then you will carry on together.
- *"Three children ..." I could either say 'We three children' or just 'We' here. I think I'll cross out 'Three children' and write 'We'.*
- Change 'they' to 'we' but leave 'their'. *There you are ... have I got it right?* See if children spot the pronoun you have missed.

Supported composition

- Give each child Copymasters C41–42.
- Continue changing the rest of the chapter plan to the first person – one chapter at a time so that you can check children's changes.
- List first person pronouns used: we, us, our. Ask children what pronouns would be used if it was the first person singular i.e. I, me, my.

Teacher scribing

- Show children the first paragraph you wrote in the previous unit and say that you are going to change it from the third to the first person.
- Explain that you want them to tell you where changes will need to be made but NOT to tell you what those changes will be.
- Underline as in the Shared Writing Example opposite.

Shared Writing Example:

"Wow, look at that!" xxxx cried. "What a fantastic old house!" They were all excited. It was the end of their journey and now the children had their first sight of the house that was to be their home for the next few weeks. They could see the evening sun shining on the windows and a smiling woman waiting for them on the steps in front of the huge door.

- Say that you are going to change it from the third person plural to the first person singular because you've decided that there will be only one child in the story. *What's the first change I need to make?* (I cried)
- *What do I need to change 'They' to? Yes, 'I'. Read that sentence for me. Yes, that's not right is it. Sometimes you have to change the verb as well as the pronoun. So what shall I write instead of 'were'?* If none of the children pick up 'all', point out that you can't say 'all' because there is only one child telling the story.
- Continue with the rest of the piece.

Independent Writing

- Individuals/pairs/groups (depending on the amount of support needed) choose an example of their own third person writing to work on – e.g. the chapters written in the previous Unit. They rewrite a section as a first person account, having decided whether it should be singular or plural. Children should swap work with someone else for checking.

Checking Children's Learning

- Do children understand what is meant by first/third person and singular or plural?
- Do they understand what a pronoun is and why it is used?
- Can they change a piece of writing from third to first person? With what degree of consistency?

Revisiting the Objective

- Choose something else in the Resource Book to change from third to first person e.g. *I Spy …* on pages 11 to 13.

Term 3 Unit of work 17:

Write sound effect poems

Resource Book pages 44–45

Writing objective:
T15: To write poetry that uses sound to create effects

Text Copymasters: C43–44

Discussing the Text

- Read the two poems.
- Establish that the point of them is to play with the sounds of words to create effects.
- *Which poem is a tongue twister? What does this mean? Rhymes like this use alliteration. What does that mean?*
- *Which words has the poet made up in the extract from 'Mud'? Why?*

Shared Writing

Session 1
Teacher demonstration

- Tell children that you are going to write two poems of your own based on the ones you have read and that you will start with the easier one, a tongue twister in the same form as Peter Piper.
- *I need a name to begin with so I'm going to have Lily Lockett and then I'm going to write 'licked a … lump of … lemon lolly.'* Pause in between as if thinking.

Teacher scribing

- Tell children to look at the Peter Piper model so they can tell you what to write next.
- Finish the poem up to the question. *I think I'm going to add something here to answer the question. I'm going to write 'She dropped it! Aaaaaaah!" What do you think? Does that improve my poem?*

Supported composition

- *Let's do another one. This time the name we're going to use is Charlie Chambers.* Write down: Charlie Chambers .... a .... of .... *So we're going to need words beginning with 'ch' to fill these spaces.*
- Ask for suggestions e.g. chips, chose, cheese.
- Tell the children to think about those words and then write their first line.
- Share and check some of the examples.
- Take suggestions for an extra line similar to the one you wrote for Lily Lockett (see Shared Writing Example). Ask the children to write one of them for their own poem.
- Take turns to say some of the tongue twisters.

Session 2
Teacher demonstration

- Have page 44 of the Resource Book visible and tell the children that you are going to write the first line of a poem about jelly based on the one about mud. (see example).

- Ask for and list words which could be used to describe jelly – what it looks like, how it moves. Start them off with 'slithers'.

Teacher scribing

- Take suggestions for the second line, having given children 30 seconds or so to discuss in pairs first. Discuss and select the line to write.
- Repeat with the remaining lines, encouraging children to make up a nonsense word for the final rhyme at least.

Shared Writing Examples:

Lily Lockett

Lily Lockett licked a lump of lemon lolly.
Did Lily Lockett lick a lump of lemon lolly?
If Lily Lockett licked a lump of lemon lolly,
Where's the lump of lemon lolly
Lily Lockett licked?
She dropped it! Aaaaaaaah!

Charlie Chambers

Charlie Chambers chewed a chunk of cherry chocolate.
Did Charlie Chambers chew a chunk of cherry chocolate?
If Charlie Chambers chewed a chunk of cherry chocolate,
Where's the chunk of cherry chocolate
Charlie Chambers chewed?
It's all gone! Mmmmmmm!

Jelly

It slips and it shivers
A wobbling blob
A slide of wet jiggles
That slithers in flobs.

Independent Writing

- Children write out the whole of their Charlie Chambers rhymes.
- They write another one using different alliteration e.g. Simon Simpson or Tina/Terry Trotter.
- In pairs, they try writing a second verse for the jelly poem.

Checking Children's Learning

- How well were the children able to use alliteration?
- How successful were they at inventing jelly-sounding nonsense words and maintaining the rhyming pattern?

Revisiting the Objective

- Write another tongue twister e.g. Sibyl Spencer sipped a spoon of spicy soup … She spat it out! Uuuuuuuugh!

Term 3 Unit of work 18:

Plan a space adventure story

Resource Book pages 46–47

Writing objective:

T10: To plot a sequence of episodes modelled on a known story as a plan for writing

Text Copymaster: C45

Discussing the Text

- Introduce the text and say that it is a plan for a story which they will already know. Read through the plan together.
- Tell the children they are going to use this plan but change things and bring them into the present day and make it into an adventure story where Jack swaps something for a tiny spaceship.

Shared Writing

Teacher scribing

- Use acetate to annotate the page. Tell children you are going to start by looking at the characters. *We might want to add things about characters to make it more up to date …* (see Shared Writing Example below). *If Jack is going into space instead of up a beanstalk, do we still need a giant? Who or what could Jack meet instead?* Delete 'giant' and write e.g. 'an alien monster'.
- *What about the settings? What would we need to change here?* Annotate the text accordingly (see Shared Writing Example).
- *Now let's think about the opening to the story. We can keep the first part but I think we need to change 'cow'. What could Jack and his mum sell instead?* Take/give suggestions e.g. Jack's old mountain bike, their television, Jack's mum's necklace etc. Select and change the sentence accordingly.

Shared Writing Example:

Characters:
Jack, a teenager who is space mad
His mother, who has lost her job
A mysterious old man
An alien monster

Settings:
Jack's house and garden; a street market; an alien planet

Opening:
Jack's mother is complaining they are poor so she suggests that Jack sells his old mountain bike which he no longer uses.

Main Events:
1. Jack is on his way to the bike shop when he meets a strange old man who asks him why he is wheeling his bike. Jack explains and the old man says he will swap the bike for the tiny silver spaceship pinned to his cloak. Jack agrees.

Teacher demonstration

- *Now we need to plan the main events for our story. There isn't enough room to write here so I'll use paper/the board. I'll start you off with the first one.* Write the first event as in the Shared Writing Example. Ask children to read it with you. Are they happy with what you have written?

Supported composition

- *In the original story, Jack takes the beans home to his mother but she is so cross that she tells him off and throws the beans out of the window. Do we want to change that for our story or keep it the same?* Write down what you and the children decide.
- *In the night, the beanstalk grows. Will the same sort of thing happen in our story?* Write down what you and the children decide.
- Plan the next event where Jack lands on an alien planet. Point out that Jack needs to find something which is <u>worth</u> taking and which he is <u>able</u> to take. It could be that he sees strange trees with leaves of gold, or diamonds placed in the bed of a stream. Discuss possibilities and then ask children to write their suggested event on their whiteboards. Select two or three examples and ask the class to vote on which one they think you should write on the plan.
- Finish planning the main events including Jack being chased/caught by (and then escaping from) the alien monster. Have children write their suggestions each time.
- Go through all the main events deciding where you will make new chapter breaks. Some will be bracketed together to make one chapter, others could make a chapter on their own.
- Decide on an ending to the story, similar to that in the model.

Independent Writing

- The children work in pairs to plan a story based on Goldilocks and the Three Bears. In this Goldilocks is out in her spaceship and spots a planet on which she decides to land. They could either use Copymaster C7 or write their own headings.

Checking Children's Learning

- How well have the children understood the need to keep to the essential bones of the original story when planning their own versions?
- *What did you find difficult in planning the story?*
- *Did planning the story make you want to write it?*

Revisiting the Objective

- Plan a similar story in which a present day Jack swaps something for a model time machine which grows and takes him back to Sherwood Forest and Robin Hood.

Term 3 Unit of work 19:

Write a chapter opening

Resource Book pages 46–47

Writing objective:

T11: To write openings to stories or chapters … to focus on language to create effects

Links to sentence/word level work

S5: How sentences can be joined in more complex ways

Text Copymaster: C45

Discussing the Text

- Look at the main events on page 47 of the Resource Book.
- Discuss how and where chapter breaks might be made in a telling of this story; for example, a short chapter each for the first two bullet points.
- Look at what would be the second chapter and discuss what it might contain. Discuss which aspect (the climb or finding the castle) would be the more interesting and therefore needs greater emphasis in the chapter.

Shared Writing

Session 1
Teacher demonstration

- Tell children that you are going to write the start of Chapter 2.
- Write Shared Writing Example 1.
- Ask the children if they think it is a very good opening to the chapter which readers would find really interesting. Hopefully they will say no! Tell them you are going to work on it to make it more interesting.
- *What does this opening tell us about the beanstalk?* (simply that it was a long way to the top). *What it was like climbing up it?* (It doesn't tell us.) *I need to say more about each of those things.*
- Discuss what the beanstalk would be like e.g. thick trunk like a tree, smaller branches, large flat leaves, small curling tendrils.
- Write Shared Writing Example 2 leaving good spacing so you can edit as per Shared Writing Example 3.
- Read what you have written aloud and ask children what you have done to make it better (e.g. added a lot more detail, given some idea of what it was like to climb a giant beanstalk).
- *I'm just going to read it through once more to see if I can make what I've written even better.* Make the changes in Shared Writing Example 3 opposite as you read e.g. second sentence: *I think I could add a couple more adjectives here …* fourth sentence*: I think it would be better if I said that the beanstalk seemed to be helping him … I don't want to repeat 'thick' so I'll say 'welcoming' because it must have been a bit scary climbing that high.* Fifth sentence: *I don't think I should repeat 'Sometimes' and 'seemed' so I'll put 'At other times' and 'felt' instead.*
- Read the final version together.

Session 2
Teacher scribing

- Read the work and recap on the process from the previous session.
- Go back to Shared Writing Example 1 and read the final sentence to the class. (*He jumped off and saw a very big castle.)* Tell them you are going to work together to improve it.

Shared Writing Example:

1. Jack climbed up the beanstalk. It was a long way to the top. He jumped off and saw a very big castle.
2. Jack began to climb. He pushed his way through the green leaves, holding on to the thick trunk. On and on he went. Sometimes the beanstalk helped him by holding out thick branches for his feet. Sometimes it seemed as if it wanted to catch him with its long tendrils. He climbed on until he reached the top.
3. Jack began to climb. He pushed his way through the *broad* green leaves, holding on to the thick *twisting* trunk. On and on he went. Sometimes the beanstalk *seemed to help* him by holding out ~~thick~~ *welcoming* branches for his feet. ~~Sometimes~~ At other times it ~~seemed~~ felt as if ~~it wanted~~ the *beanstalk* wanted to ~~catch~~ *trap* him with its long ~~tendrils like~~ *curling fingers*. He climbed *wearily* on until he reached the top.

- *Let's take the first part of the sentence. How do you think Jack would have felt here? Tired? Out of breath? Would he jump off or step off?* Take suggestions from the children. Compose and scribe a sentence e.g. 'Jack stepped off the beanstalk and sat down to rest for a moment.'
- Read the sentence back and ask/guide the children to improve it e.g. 'Jack stepped off the beanstalk and, because his legs felt weak after his long climb, he sat down for a moment to rest.'
- Read the second part of Shared Writing Example 1. *How can we introduce the fact that Jack sees a castle in the distance – does he stand up and look around or what?* Take suggestions then compose and scribe a sentence e.g. 'Jack got to his feet and, looking around him, saw a castle in the distance.'

Supported composition

- Children work individually or in pairs, to compose sentences about the castle with Jack seeing more and more detail as he gets closer, until he is finally standing in front of the door.

Independent Writing

- Choose another chapter and write the opening.

Checking Children's Learning

- How successfully are children able to revise their writing?
- What degree of complexity are they able to bring to their sentences?

Revisiting the Objective

- Use the same process to write the opening to the story itself.

Term 3 Unit of work 20:

Make notes and write a review

Resource Book page 48

Writing Composition Objective:
T14: to write book reviews for a specified audience, based on evaluations of plot, characters and language.

Text Copymaster: C46

Discussing the Text

- Reread the story of The Ant and the Grasshopper on pages 26–29.
- Read the story aloud. Discuss the characters, setting and the moral.
- Ask children to identify the author's use of imaginative comparisons on page 28 and discuss the effectiveness of the images.
- What other points can children make about the author's writing? (E.g. the one word sentences 'Summer.' 'Winter.' for impact.

Shared Writing

Teacher Demonstration

- Turn to Copymaster C46. Tell children that you are going to make notes here to help everyone write a proper review of the story later on. Refer back to the story if necessary at any point.
- *I'm going to start with what the story is about. Remember I'm just making notes so the first thing I'll put is: retelling of Aesop's Fable.*
- Continue with the notes as in Shared Writing Example 1.
- *My opinion of the way the characters are described … I think the author describes them very well so I'm going to put …* As Example 2; comment on the use of a quotation from the text to prove a point and the way it is punctuated. *What else could I mention?* Take suggestions and scribe as notes.

Teacher Scribing

- Ask for children's comments about the ending of the story. If opinion is divided draw a line down the middle of the available space and head the left-hand side 'Some people think that …' and the right-hand side 'Other people think that …' Scribe views in note form.

Supported Composition

- Have a short discussion on whether or not children would recommend the story to someone else and their reasons for this.
- Ask the children to note their recommendation and the reasons for it on their whiteboards. Stress that there is no need to write in sentences – they are only writing notes for later use.
- Share some of the children's views and reasons, scribing them in note form as you do so.
- Read through all the review notes and see if there is anything which needs to be added to any of the sections.

Shared Writing Example:

1. Retelling of Aesop's fable
   Moral: Thrift and hard work – the secret of success!
   Summer – Ant busy storing food, Grasshopper doesn't bother – plays cello
   Winter – Grasshopper has no food – goes to Ant – Ant refuses to help
2. described v. well – use of imaginative comparisons e.g. 'thin as wire, legs all out of tune' – makes characters seem real
3. The story is a retelling of one of Aesop's fables with the moral: 'Thrift and hard work – the secret of success!' It tells how during the summer Ant is busy storing food for the winter.

Teacher Demonstration

- Tell children that they are going to write their own reviews of the story based on the notes you have done together. *This means that you will have to turn the notes into proper sentences. I'm going to do a bit of the writing* (on paper or the board) *to show you how.*
- Read the notes from Shared Writing Example 1 … 'Retelling of Aesop's fable'. *I can't leave it like this so I'm going to write 'The story is a retelling of one of Aesop's fables' and then I'm going to add 'with the moral 'Thrift and hard work – the secret of success!' I could have had two sentences but I think it is better as one. Notice how I've put quotes around the moral.*
- Finish writing Shared Writing Example 3.

Independent Writing

- Children write their own reviews. Ensure the notes and your opening from the Shared Writing are visible. Children could use Text Copymaster C46 for this, but the more able children at least should write their reviews in paragraphs without headings – other than the story title and author.

Checking Children's Learning

- How successful were children in writing notes during supported composition?
- How successfully have they translated notes into complete sentences?
- Do reviews written without headings include sections on plot, character description, the ending and personal views of the story? Have any quotes been used to support statements?

Revisiting the Objective

- Write a review of another story the children know or use the extract from Cinderella on page 32 of the Resource Book.

Describing Settings

C1

Place	Time of day	Weather	Sights	Sounds	Smells
Funfair					
School Playground					
A River					
City Street					
Fairy Tale Palace					

What Kind of Ending Is It?

C2

- Says something about the way the character feels:

- Adds some descriptive details about the setting:

- Says that the character has changed or learned something:

- The author 'speaks' to the reader directly:

- Says something about the future:

- Ends with a question:

Key Incidents Flow chart

C3

Write Your Own Verse

C4

My ....

My .... of ....

Has seven .... as ....

Who sit ....

And watch ....

....

....

The firelight leaps, the parlour glows,

And, while the music ebbs and flows,

They .... (while ....)

....

A Story Plan

C5

Title:

Character list:

•

Settings:

Starts with:

Moves to:

Introduction:

Main Events:

•

Ending:

Character Notes

Character 1 **Name:**	**Character 2** **Name:**	**Situation and how they feel about each other**
What I know from the text or illustrations:	What I know from the text or illustrations:	What I know from the text or illustrations:
What I can also imagine:	What I can also imagine:	What I can also imagine:

Planning a Story

C7

Characters:

Settings:

What the story could be about:

Opening:

Main events:

-

Ending:

Possible title:

Describing Settings

An Autumn Wood

Dusk, and the warm, damp and earthy smell of Autumn was in the air. The rain dripped slowly from the yellowing leaves as if the trees themselves were weeping at the passing of Summer. Trees were shedding their tears. Just as soon they would shed their dying leaves.

Unit of work 1

The Castle

He stopped. There was the castle in front of him with its walls and towers stretching up towards a cloudless sky.

He smiled. It seemed like the castle was straining to reach the sun ... trying to warm its old, granite bones. Narrow windows winked at him and the drawbridge was down to welcome him home.

A Grey Day

The beach was deserted now for who would want to brave those icy, biting winds and the wild, whipping waves? There were no laughing children, no sandcastles, no sleeping dads and no deckchairs.

In fact, there was no colour – just grey skies above a grey sea beginning a grey day!

City Spring

People on their way to work seem
to have a spring in their step as if
they are cheered by the daffodils
smiling through park railings, the
displays of Easter eggs behind
sunlit windows and the fresh leaves
of green in the tree-lined roads.
Spring. Even the word sounds right
for the time of year!

Wendy Body

Unit of work 1

Writing Dialogue

The characters:

- Mr Simpkins is a tall, thin man with neat grey hair and faded blue eyes. He is rather short-tempered and lives alone – except for his dog. He doesn't go out much, but he is often seen pottering about in his garden.
- Marcus lives next door and is ten years old. He has red hair, freckles and a cheeky grin. He is a real chatterbox who loves reading and playing football.
- Kerry is Marcus' rather sensible eight-year-old sister. She has long auburn hair and wears glasses. She likes gardening, reading comics, and is as good at football as her brother.

The Conversation

Marcus and Kerry stood by Mr Simpkins' shiny red front door.
"Hey! Do you think he's a Man United fan?" whispered Marcus.

Kerry giggled and then hissed, "Knock on the door, Marcus!"
"No! You do it!" Marcus replied.

Kerry took a deep breath and knocked on Mr Simpkins' door.

Imaginative Comparisons

The one who displays toes
like archway windows
bringing the pads of her feet down
like giant paperweights
to keep the earth from shifting about.

From a poem about an elephant by Grace Nichols called: *For Dilberta*

The reader of this poem
Is as cracked as a cup
As daft as treacle toffee
As mucky as a pup.

From *The Reader of This Poem* by Roger McGough

He'd a huge black overcoat.
He felt proud in it.
You could have hidden
A football crowd in it.

From *Grandad* by Kit Wright

As she came closer I could see that her black fur was tipped with white. It was as if it were midnight and the moon were shining on her fur, frosting it.

From *The Midnight Fox* by Betsy Byars

Her face was white – not merely pale, but white like snow or paper or icing-sugar, except for her very red mouth.

From *The Lion, the Witch and the Wardrobe* by C. S. Lewis

At that very moment – ears flying, feet thumping, fast as a speeding bullet – the hare hurtled over the finish line.

From *The Hare and the Tortoise* by Geraldine McCaughrean in "Aesop's Fables"

Short story: I Spy ...

Megan was bored. David was even more bored. "Dad, are we nearly there yet?" he whined.

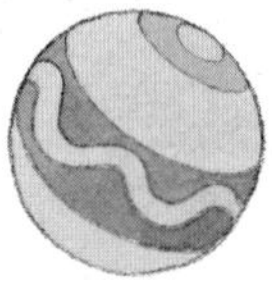

This was the tenth time that David had asked the same question.
"I'm getting fed up with you!" said Megan, giving her brother a shove.

Dad sighed and then said, "Look, it's bad enough driving for two hours without having to listen to you two arguing."

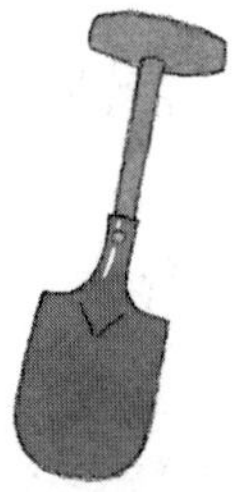

Mum told the children to be quiet and find something to do. Megan replied that not only had she finished reading her comics but she had also done all the puzzles in her book.

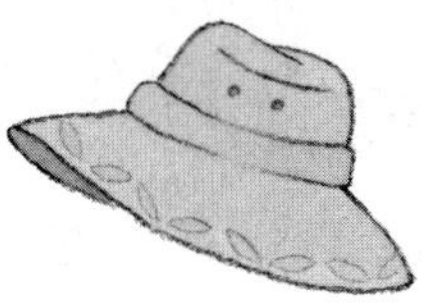

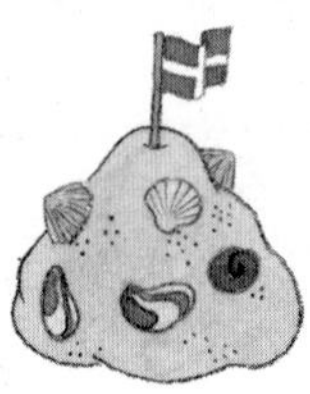

"I've read my comic too AND I've listened to my story tapes," complained David.

"O.K. then, let's play *I Spy* for a while," said Mum. "You start, Megan."

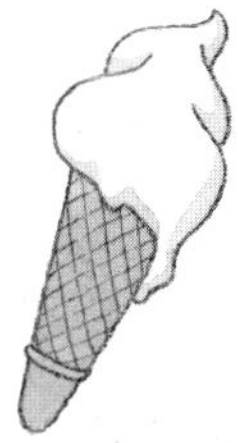

Megan grinned. "I spy with my little eye something beginning with F."

They had several goes but no-one could guess. Finally, David asked her what it was.

"F is for FOOL!" said Megan, giggling and pointing at her brother.

Mum told Megan off so Megan said she was sorry to David and told him that it was his turn next.

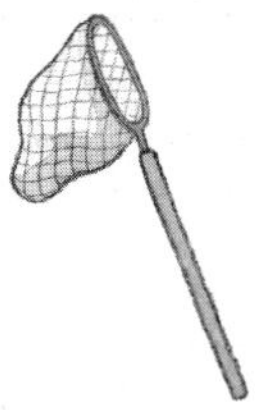

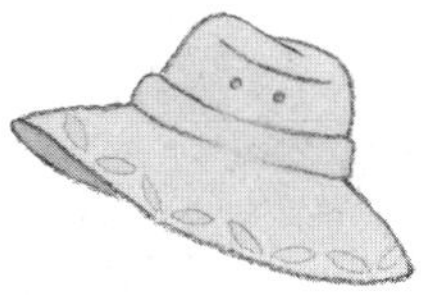

Units of work 4 and 5

The problem was that David wasn't too sure of his alphabet and had them looking for something beginning with G when he was thinking of "jumper"!

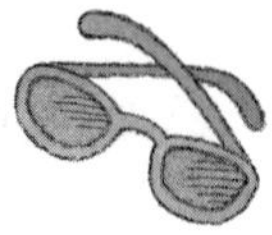

Suddenly, Dad slowed down and opened the window. "Look everybody!" he said, pointing. "I spy with my little eye something beginning with S ... . It's the sea and we're here at last!"

Wendy Body

Units of work 4 and 5

Shape Poems

Sleeping

Lamp-post
There is simply nothing
that my dog
Merlin
likes
more
than
to
stop
at a
nice
tall
grey
lamp-
post
when
he is
out
for a
walk!
Wendy Body
Unit of work 6

Unit of work 6

Unit of work 6

Openings

It was a stormy night with clouds that growled their way across the thundery sky.

Tales on a Cold Dark Night by Linda Strachan

Long ago and far away in Russia, near to a great forest, lived Peter with his grandfather.

A Pack of Wolf Tales by Ann Jungman

On a misty-soft island morning when the early sun played with the dew on the grass, Estelle walked across the fields to her home.

Estelle's Reward by Wendy Body

One day, a duck tried on an egg-shell as a hat.

The Duck in the Hat by Martin Waddell

This is the story of Yim Sung, a poor Chinese fisherman who had no wife, no money and no food.

The Turtle Who Danced with the Crane by Stan Cullimore

Tom Murphy was young when his father was hung.

Poor Tom and the Smugglers of Mourne by Martin Waddell

Endings

They called him "Lightning" after that. But the names they thought up for that silly hare I won't repeat.

The Hare and the Tortoise by Geraldine McCaughrean

The little pig enjoyed the soup for several days and from then on lived happily ever after in his strong brick house.

A Pack of Wolf Tales by Ann Jungman

Robin sank to his knees on the cool damp moss. He was safe in the welcoming wood once more.

Wendy Body

Unit of work 7

Tinker did not go exploring again. The world beyond her home was too uncertain, too dangerous. "No," she thought contentedly, "this is where I want to be."

Wendy Body

Later that day, Ranjit sat and stared out through the rain-spattered window. After everything that had happened, could his life ever be the same again?

Wendy Body

Writing a Story in Paragraphs

Title:

Paragraph 1:
Introduce the setting and main characters: two children are walking their dog in the woods.

Paragraph 2:
Give more information about the characters – their names, relationship and appearances.

Unit of work 8

Paragraphs 3 and 4:
Mainly dialogue: the two children are chatting about school when the dog finds something and starts barking at it.

Paragraph 5:
The children discover that the dog has found an injured bird.

Paragraph 6:
They discuss what they might do – leave it, take it home and look after it, take it to a bird sanctuary – but they reject these ideas.

Paragraph 7:
They decide to take it home and get their mum to go to the local vet with them. They catch the bird.

Paragraph 8:
Mum agrees. They find something to put the bird in and walk to the vet's surgery.

Unit of work 8

Paragraph 9:
The vet explains that she will treat the bird and keep it until it can be released.

Paragraph 10:
Mum and the children are walking home when the dog starts barking at something under a hedge ...

Ant and Grasshopper

Summer. The Grasshopper played the cello with her back legs, and basked in the warmth. "What you a-doing, Ant," she asked, "always bustling about?"

"Busy, busy, busy," said the Ant racing past with a grain of wheat. "Preparing for winter. So should you."

"Later, later," groaned the Grasshopper. "Who wants to think about winter in the summertime?" And her antennae waved in time to her music.

Units of work 9, 10 and 20

Winter. The grass was pin-stiff with frost, but deep below it the Ant rested cosy in his nest. The shelves were lined with food, so were the cellars and lofts. A live-in larder.

Someone came knocking at the Ant's door. "Oh, spare me a bite to eat, neighbour!" wailed the Grasshopper, thin as wire, legs all out of tune.

"You should have thought of that in the summer!" shouted the Ant through his letterbox. "I warned you. Now you must pay for your gallivanting!" And back he went, to sit out winter in his great, silent larder.

Geraldine McCaughrean

Units of work 9, 10 and 20

My Uncle Paul of Pimlico

My Uncle Paul of Pimlico
Has seven cats as white as snow,
Who sit at his enormous feet
And watch him, as a special treat,
Play the piano upside-down,
In his delightful dressing gown;
The firelight leaps, the parlour glows,
And, while the music ebbs and flows,
They smile (while purring
   the refrains),
At little thoughts that cross
   their brains.

Mervyn Peake

Unit of work 11

Cinderella

Suddenly there was a puff of smoke, a flash of light and a fairy godmother appeared.

She smiled and said:
"Oh, Cinderella, don't be sad,
It really *isn't* all that bad.
My magic wand will set things right –
You *shall* go to the ball tonight!"

With that, the fairy godmother waved her magic wand. Cinderella's tattered old clothes immediately changed into a beautiful dress and her scruffy old shoes became a pair of delicate glass slippers.
"What lovely slippers!" said Cinderella. "Thank you." Then she frowned. "But how am I going to get to the palace?"

The fairy godmother smiled, then pointed her wand at a pumpkin. It changed into a magnificent coach.

Then the fairy waved her wand at the mice. They squeaked and grew and squeaked and grew and soon – they had grown into two fine horses!

Then the fairy godmother said:
"Now Cinderella, although I'm clever,
The carriage and horses won't
last forever!
When the clock strikes twelve at the
ball tonight,
Come home at once – or you'll be a
sorry sight!"

So Cinderella jumped into the carriage and went to the ball.

from *Cinderella* by Stan Cullimore

Unit of work 12

Writing Character Portraits

Unit of work 13

Unit of work 13

Plan the Story

The Main Characters:

- a girl
- a woman
- a dragon
- a dwarf

The Settings:

- a house

What the story could be about:

Opening:

Unit of work 14

Main Events:

Ending:

Possible Titles:

Unit of work 14

Writing a Story in Chapters

Chapter 1

Three children go to stay with an aunt they have never met while their parents are away. She is the caretaker of a stately home.

Chapter 2

The next day she sends them off to explore the house. They finish up in a dusty old attic where one of the children discovers an old book.

Chapter 3

The book turns out to be a diary kept by the mistress of the house. They find an entry which describes how she has hidden her jewels under one of the

Units of work 15 and 16

stones in the floor of the summer-house. She is frightened of her husband and plans to run away.

Chapter 4

The children show their aunt the diary. The summer-house no longer exists but, on an old map of the grounds, they find where it used to be.

Chapter 5

They search and eventually find the old stones beneath the grass. They get them up and start digging. It looks as if they won't find anything and then one of them hits metal.

Chapter 6

They discover a rusty old box. They break it open and find ...

Units of work 15 and 16

Mud

It squelches and belches
A spattering flop
A morass of dense goop
That gurges in glops

Now seeping now weeping
A popple a spurt
A lagoon of brown pudding
Some very wet dirt

Zaro Weil

Peter Piper

Peter Piper picked a peck of
pickled pepper;
Did Peter Piper pick a peck of
pickled pepper?
If Peter Piper picked a peck of
pickled pepper
Where's the peck of pickled pepper
Peter Piper picked?

Anon

Jack and the Beanstalk: a story plan

Characters:
- Jack, a teenager
- Jack's mother
- a mysterious old man
- a giant

Settings:
- Jack's cottage and garden
- the market
- the giant's castle

Opening:
Jack's mother tells him they are so poor that they must sell their cow.

Main Events:
- Jack exchanges the cow for some magic beans which grow into a huge beanstalk.
- He climbs up the beanstalk and finds the giant's castle.
- He steals from the giant.
- The giant chases Jack but he escapes down the beanstalk.
- Jack chops the beanstalk down while the giant is still on it.

Ending:
Jack and his mum are rich because of the goose which lays golden eggs that Jack stole from the giant.

Units of work 18 and 19